the beat

goes on

First published in Great Britain in 1999 by **Granada Media**
an imprint of André Deutsch Ltd
in association with Granada Media Group
76 Dean Street
London W1V 5HA

www.vci.co.uk

Design and layout by Essential Books

Printed and Bound in Great Britain by Butler & Tanner Ltd.

A catalogue record for this book is available from the British Library

ISBN 0 233 99716 4

Exposed the tube

Maria Malone

GRANADA
MEDIA
Consumer Products

For Sarah

The one thing that can be said for *The Tube* crowd is that they are singularly the sweetest, most generous, most reliable people in the entire world. I am eternally grateful to all those who helped me with this book.

I am especially appreciative of the beautiful and gifted Paula Yates and the immensely talented and devastatingly attractive Jools Holland.

From the very outset Andrea Wonfor proved an inspiration, as did Geoff Wonfor, creative genius that he is.

Malcolm Gerrie, who did so much to change the face of music television, provided anecdotes and encouragement. (Mind those heady cocktails, kid.)

Thanks also to Chris Cowey, source of wonderful stories, and a truly exceptional individual.

I am grateful to Gavin Taylor whose innovative style in Studio 5 made such a splash, and to Chris Phipps, one of the most astute talent-spotters in the business.

Thanks also to Adam Clayton and Paul McGuinness, to Vic Reeves, Peter York and Norman Pace.

There were many others who squeezed me into their busy schedules, among them Sir Jeremy Isaacs, Andy Allen, Paul Corley, Mike Bolland, Michael Metcalf, John Gwyn, Colin Rowell, Ged Doherty, Andy McDonald, Trevor Horn and Andy Harries.

Thanks also to Graham Diss who manfully ploughed through a pile of tapes in the early stages of the project.

Geordie hospitality and support came courtesy of Margaret Fay and her team at Tyne Tees Television. Meanwhile, Ingrid Connell and Deborah Waight at André Deutsch proved pillars of strength throughout.

With love to Sharon Jane Thomas, who wisely counselled against a warm bath with a sharp razor blade, and to Linda Barker for being there.

Finally, a big thank you to Valerie.

Acknowledgements

4

CONTENTS

foreword

I HAVE ENJOYED ENORMOUSLY looking through Maria Malone's excellent book on *The Tube*. It is a beautifully-crafted, affectionate work which will add lustre and style to any home or office. This book has, in many ways, caught the spirit of *The Tube*. Its pages, like the programmes themselves, are filled with spontaneity, humour, a love of music, and bare-faced lies.

There were a number of wonderful things that happened during the making of *The Tube*. Firstly, it did an excellent job of hijacking television from the professionals and grown-ups and created a spontaneous world of jaunty camera angles that is still with us today. Secondly, we got to make lots of films and make friends with people all around the world. Many of them still write to me. Obviously I never reply. I have never actually seen any of these programmes, but I am told they are very good.

I insist you purchase this book, or if you are unable to do so, you steal it.

I have the honour to remain your obedient servant.

PS. Any money I receive from the proceeds of this book will be donated to the Tyne Tees Benevolent Society.

by Jools Holland

Tube director Geoff Wonfor and Paula Yates in Paris. Or is it Blackpool?

Introduction

IT WAS AN UNSUSPECTING AUDIENCE that tuned in to watch the first ever *Tube* in the autumn of 1982. The show was unlike anything seen on television before. It was brash and messy (on purpose). It had a wild, anarchic air. It had the best bands. And it was live. From the very beginning the viewers were hooked. *The Tube* had made its mark and would continue to do so for the next five years.

It was during the planning stages for the new Channel 4 that the idea of *The Tube* was born. Chief Executive Jeremy Isaacs felt that an early-evening music show would provide a cornerstone in the new channel's schedule. He was looking for something innovative which, in its own unique style, would recapture the spirit of a Sixties show he remembered fondly – *Ready, Steady, Go!*

The task to devise a suitable show went to Tyne Tees Television, who'd made a number of successful regional music and youth programmes. Initially, they envisioned six hour-long shows (recorded) with the working title *Jamming*. Isaacs was blunt. It had to be live. It had to be long. And it would run for 20 weeks. Controversially, the new show would also come from Newcastle.

No one could have predicted the impact of *The Tube*, which aired just a few days after Channel 4 launched. It set its own distinctive agenda and demonstrated a whole new way of making television. With a weekly audience of around a million, *The Tube* rapidly became one of the new channel's flagship shows. Early into the first series Channel 4 commissioned a *Tube* special. A second series followed – 25 episodes this time. In all, *The Tube* ran for five series and notched up an incredible 121 shows, plus specials, before it finally came to an end in April 1987. It was an extraordinary success story.

Much of that success was down to Jools Holland and Paula Yates, who were utterly unlike the slick breed of presenters so typical of the time. They made mistakes, they forgot the

names of the bands, they looked at the wrong camera. Nonetheless, they were the epitome of cool. And there existed between them a chemistry that positively crackled. Many people mistakenly thought they were a couple. Jools once said they had become like a television husband and wife team – but a husband and wife team you only expected the worst of.

When Paula left at the end of the first series to have her first child, Fifi, Leslie Ash stepped in as her replacement. Leslie, a model and actress, was new to presenting. She stayed for just one series. Accomplished as she was, Leslie never appeared quite as laid-back amid the mayhem of *The Tube* as her predecessor. When the third series began in October '84 Paula was back where she belonged – in Studio 5 with Jools.

What made *The Tube* so remarkable is that it somehow found a lasting place deep in the psyche of its audience. For the generation who grew up with the show, quite simply there was no show before or after to rival it. Those who knew *The Tube* look back on it with enormous affection. It was their show. It signalled the start of the weekend. The audience – whether in the studio or at home – felt part of the whole experience.

It was influential, too. For five years *The Tube* was a platform for new bands, many of whom – like Frankie Goes To Hollywood and Fine Young Cannibals – became massively successful. For established bands, an appearance on the show sent record sales soaring. It was a brave – or feckless – record company executive who failed to switch on the TV at 5.15pm on Fridays. In retrospect, *The Tube* threw the dice and won. It experimented. It broke new ground. Sometimes it went badly wrong, but nobody really cared.

The odd mishap paled into insignificance compared with the many great bands that played live, the endless moments of sheer madness, and the show's capacity for eclectic line-ups. Only *The Tube* would put Public Image Limited on the same show as Tina Turner. Or Killing Joke with Cliff Richard.

In the end, testimony to the success of *The Tube* must rest with the artists who appeared on the show ... U2, REM, Simple Minds, David Bowie, Elton John, Iggy Pop, Duran Duran, Little Richard, Dr John, Jam, Eurythmics... and hundreds more besides.

> '**It genuinely was good when it was good but that was just by chance.**'
>
> Paula Yates

One:
In the Beginning

5 NOVEMBER, 1982. BONFIRE NIGHT. Jools Holland stands in the rain outside the Tyne Tees studios on City Road in Newcastle. Behind him a pink neon sign bearing the word *Tube* glows in the darkness above the futuristic tunnel leading into the building. On his left a bedraggled queue shelters under umbrellas, waiting for the doors to open to Studio 5, where a new live music show is about to make its debut. 'We're going to do something new that's going to go down in the annals of TV history,' he declares. 'You're going to see live bands so remember, turn it up – from now on you'll be watching fantastic *Tube*.'

Someone thrusts a sparkler into his hand and the opening titles roll. The Jam, Heaven 17, Sting, Pete Townshend. Inside Studio 5 a pregnant Paula Yates, radiant in a short frothy confection of a dress with matching pink bow on her microphone, picks her way through a scene dock strewn with cables. 'For the next five months you're going to be seeing live music, interviews, my stomach getting bigger. In fact things that have never been seen before on a live TV show.'

The tone may have been firmly tongue-in-cheek but the sentiment was to prove entirely accurate. From the word go *The Tube* was different from any other programme on television. There had been nothing quite like it. Where others were slick and safe *The Tube* went out of its way to be raw and anarchic.

Having decided to split, The Jam played the first *Tube* on 5 November, 1982. It was their final TV appearance

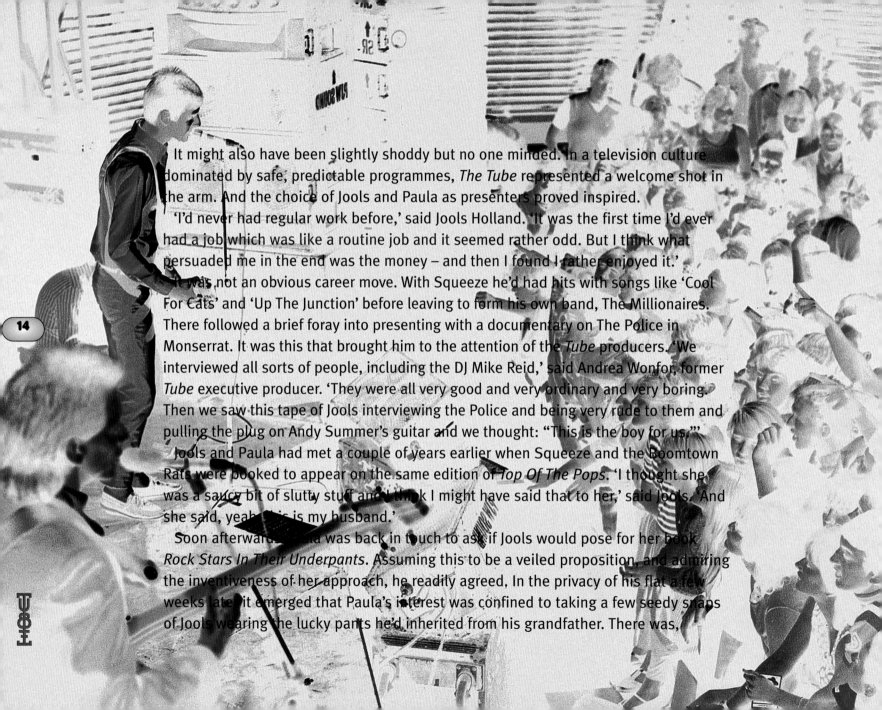

It might also have been slightly shoddy but no one minded. In a television culture dominated by safe, predictable programmes, *The Tube* represented a welcome shot in the arm. And the choice of Jools and Paula as presenters proved inspired.

'I'd never had regular work before,' said Jools Holland. 'It was the first time I'd ever had a job which was like a routine job and it seemed rather odd. But I think what persuaded me in the end was the money – and then I found I rather enjoyed it.'

It was not an obvious career move. With Squeeze he'd had hits with songs like 'Cool For Cats' and 'Up The Junction' before leaving to form his own band, The Millionaires. There followed a brief foray into presenting with a documentary on The Police in Monserrat. It was this that brought him to the attention of the *Tube* producers. 'We interviewed all sorts of people, including the DJ Mike Reid,' said Andrea Wonfor, former *Tube* executive producer. 'They were all very good and very ordinary and very boring. Then we saw this tape of Jools interviewing the Police and being very rude to them and pulling the plug on Andy Summer's guitar and we thought: "This is the boy for us."'

Jools and Paula had met a couple of years earlier when Squeeze and the Boomtown Rats were booked to appear on the same edition of *Top Of The Pops*. 'I thought she was a saucy bit of slutty stuff and I think I might have said that to her,' said Jools. 'And she said, yeah, this is my husband.'

Soon afterwards Paula was back in touch to ask if Jools would pose for her book *Rock Stars In Their Underpants*. Assuming this to be a veiled proposition, and admiring the inventiveness of her approach, he readily agreed, In the privacy of his flat a few weeks later it emerged that Paula's interest was confined to taking a few seedy snaps of Jools wearing the lucky pants he'd inherited from his grandfather. There was, however, some consolation. 'When she photographed me she did it in a bikini, which I thought was rather good,' he said. 'And then she felt ill and I had to take her round to my mother's house for a Beecham's Powder or something. I don't know if it was the effect of seeing me in my pantaloons.'

'I can't get in a car without getting really sick,' said Paula. 'I remember going all the way to Greenwich and just getting out of the car at his mother's house and just spewing, *spraying* the front garden. And I lay there face down, just broken, and his mother came out and kneeled down and gave me a Penguin biscuit – I knew Jools really well from that day on.'

Paula came to the notice of Tyne Tees when she guested on a regional youth show, *Check It Out*, to promote her book. Appropriately, presenter Chris Cowey – who went on to become a researcher on *The Tube* and now produces and directs *Top Of The Pops* – sported a pair of lucky underpants of his own for the interview.

Jools and Paula were invited to Tyne Tees to record a pilot edition of *The Tube*. If the producers were looking for something edgy and off-the-wall, they'd found it. 'I remember we were both pretty horrible,' said Jools. 'We said lots of unpleasant things like, "On this programme we'll be dragging someone's corpse around and sodomising someone who's boring." We had to interview some teenagers and stuff like that and we didn't like it at all.' He recalled how Paula began berating the interviewees – drafted in from a local college for what they had been promised would be a pleasant afternoon – within a few minutes of meeting them. 'She was sort of punching them, which I really thought was good, 'cos that's what they deserved,' he said.

The producers witnessed this performance with a growing conviction that Jools and

'Do you think being called Gordon has been a bit of a hindrance to being a pop star?' she said. Sting rolled his eyes in irritation. 'Yeah, it's really held me back.'

Paula were exactly what they were looking for. 'They did the most appalling audition – it was all over the place – but there was something in the chemistry and we just liked it,' said Andrea Wonfor. 'Something happened when they were together, even if they did miss their marks and couldn't remember what they were saying.'

Jools and Paula were never going to be slick, polished presenters – much to everyone's relief. But they were funny and unpredictable and somehow *right*. 'We had such a similar sense of humour. Anyway, it was made in heaven for us both,' said Paula. 'I remember we had lots of little traditions, like on the way home on Thursdays after the run-through Jools would always make me get out of the car and stand under a lamppost, then he'd go round the block and kerb crawl me. I'd be standing there like an idiot in the middle of Gosforth and he'd lean over and say, "A fiver, babes?" Then we'd go home.'

Channel 4 chief executive Jeremy Isaacs felt Jools and Paula perfectly embodied the spirit of *The Tube*. 'Paula gave her all in a terribly obvious, "Here I am," in-your-face sort of way. Jools had a wonderful mocking deadpan cool. He had a calm, hip manner and he really knew what he was talking about. And he could do it himself – he could play. I thought they were both skilled presenters,' he said.

Significantly, the producers decided there was no place for autocue. There would be no tightly-scripted links for the presenters. Instead, Jools and Paula would improvise, giving the show a loose, anything-could-happen attitude. 'Up until then there was always the same thing – a lighting gantry, some people dancing about, a couple of bands and a vaguely groovy-looking person introducing them,' said Jools.

'When we first went up to do *The Tube* I was rather disappointed to see it was a load of lighting gantries, lots of flashing lights, and young people dancing about again. I was thinking: "Is this just a lot of gantries and young people standing around like all those other shows?" But it managed to break away from that.

'At first it could have been like that with items on hairdressing and, I don't know, earnest people being concerned, but it managed to get away from that through everyone on the show realising you could make it up as you went along.'

The idea of roving cameras was introduced. On *The Tube* you could see presenters wandering along the corridors or bursting into dressing rooms. No area was sacrosanct with every part of the building used – the artists' Green Room, the toilets, the make-up room, the car park, even the two neighbouring pubs – The Egypt Cottage and The Rose And Crown. Technically, it was a huge innovation. 'We even filmed in the lift,' said director Gavin Taylor. 'New, lightweight cameras were the vogue and we decided to break new ground visually with the style of *The Tube*.'

With his neat blazers and pressed flannels, Gavin Taylor was never the archetypal rock 'n' roll director. 'Gavin looked like the chairman of the local bowls club,' recalled Andy Allen, then director of programmes at Tyne Tees. 'He was totally dapper. But he really knew how to move cameras around and that was the thing about *The Tube* – the cameras were right in there with the bands.'

The first show set the tone for what was to come. What every fan remembers is the blistering twenty-minute set from The Jam which wrapped up the programme. Eight tracks in all, including 'A Town Called Malice', 'Move On Up', and the new single 'Beat Surrender', which shot straight to Number 1 following its release a few weeks later.

It was the last television appearance by the band, following reports that they were to split. What few people knew was that they had intended to announce the break-up on *The Tube*. When news of the split broke in the *New Musical Express* there were fears publicity-shy Paul Weller would pull out of the show. 'I thought: "That's it, they won't want to do it now,"' said former producer Malcolm Gerrie. 'But it wasn't a problem. Paul still wanted to play. The element of surprise had gone, but the flipside was that everyone was dying to see them 'cos they knew it was going to be their last ever gig.'

He had tried to arrange for Who guitarist Pete Townshend to play with the band: 'I knew Paul idolised him but at that time collaborations just did not happen.' In the end, Townshend appeared as a guest, but could not be persuaded to perform.

The Jam's decision to bow out on the show was a huge coup for *The Tube*. Their set still ranks as one of the highlights of the show's five-year run. Earlier in the show, Sunderland band The Toy Dolls had kicked things off with an energetic set in the reception of Tyne Tees. While images leapt about on a bank of screens behind them, the audience filed past. It was chaotically informal. 'We were going out of our way to create something edgy, sharp and a little bit off-the-wall,' said Paul Corley, one of the original producers.

'The programme had that feeling of anarchy and attachment to a young audience. It was risky, it was ambitious – it was from Newcastle. It was the new kid on the block that had all the bands you wanted to see. It also had a lot of extra dimensions that appealed to people.'

In the studio Paula chatted to local-lad-made-good, Sting. 'Do you think being called Gordon has been a bit of a hindrance to being a pop star?' she said. Sting rolled his eyes in irritation. 'Yeah, it's really held me back,' he replied. Undeterred, Paula pressed on. 'In an interview recently you said you liked doing "it" on the kitchen table, but when I was at your house the kitchen table didn't look big enough to get more than a couple of bowls of rice on it.' Sting grinned. 'No, *that* kitchen table I gave to an institute that was studying sexual practise in Hampstead, and it's now a museum piece. Still got the marks on it.' She waved her notes at him. 'Sssssh!'

It was a welcome departure from the average exchange between pop star and presenter. Paula had started as she meant to go on.

'The good thing about *The Tube* was that before then it had all gone a bit earnest,' said Jools. 'Maybe the thing was it wasn't at all journalistic. It tried that once or twice but fell flat on its face. It was a bit more showbizzy. A lot of it was spontaneous, which people liked, as well as being messy.'

It was this messiness as much as anything that made it watchable. 'You kept thinking: "What's going to happen now? Is it going to fall apart?"' said Jools. '"Am I going to tune in and see two dogs fucking for an hour?" Something like that. People just didn't know and that's another reason people liked it.'

In his office in London Channel 4 Chief Executive Jeremy Isaacs had watched the first show with a sense of pride and disbelief.

'I couldn't believe what I saw,' he said. 'I couldn't have been given a more perfect start to the weekend. It was totally unlike any other programme I had ever seen.

'What made its impact on me immediately was the use of cameras in the studio. I still think it was sensational. They took you inside the music – they didn't stand back observing it. The cameras swung round the studio like a great swirling painting. They'd given me something wonderful and with tears in my eyes I picked up the telephone and tried to thank them.'

There was one entirely new face to television on that first show. Muriel Gray was one of five 'unknowns' selected as presenters following nationwide auditions. And she was hurled straight in at the deep end with an interview with the famously shy Paul Weller.

doing so well so far – why take the risk of spoiling it all by releasing a record?'

Muriel grills
Sigue Sigue
Sputnik

'You could have a a
sticker saying My
Other Band Are
Musicians

As Weller perched awkwardly on a bench in his dressing room Muriel did her best to coax him into conversation. She asked him about his involvement in fanzines. She asked about his gift for writing poetry. She wanted to know what plans the band had following the split. Weller proved taciturn. 'You're not going to give up music altogether, are you?' she persisted. He gazed at his feet. 'I don't think any of us will, 'cos it's in our blood, you know what I mean?' Muriel pressed him. 'Might that take a different turn? I mean what kind of involvement do you see yourself having in music?' He looked nonplussed. 'Em, how do you mean?'

She persisted. 'Well, let me rephrase that, Paul. If you're going to do music of a different type are you going to do it with different people or just branching out by yourself?' He shrugged. 'Well, I haven't thought about it really, quite honestly. Sorry about that.' 'Oh well, that's the end of that,' said Muriel. Not that it was. There was still time for more questions and tortuous answers. Later in the show she had her revenge when she introduced the band as 'those masters of wit and repartee.'

Muriel became a regular on *The Tube* but never quite hit it off with Jools and Paula. 'I remember having to kneel with Jools outside Muriel's dressing room saying "You're really good-looking, we really like you," under the door,' said Paula. 'She'd lock herself in and not want to come out just before the show. It was just like school, where one person's left out.'

As the series progressed Muriel, at the time working for the National Museum Of Antiquities in Edinburgh, developed a fearsome interview technique.

When Tony James and Martin Degville of Sigue Sigue Sputnik appeared on the show she introduced them as 'The band everyone's been reading about but no one's talking about. Now boys, you've been doing so well so far – why risk spoiling it all by releasing a record?' The Sputniks struggled manfully to maintain a degree of cool as Muriel ploughed on. 'Are you not scared you're going to be a bit like a funny car sticker – amusing the first time you look at it, then you hate it every time you see it.' Another thought occurred to her. 'You could have a sticker saying My Other Band Are Musicians.'

It was Muriel who proved the most enduring of the five newcomers. Nick Laird-Clowes, with his trademark hats, later fronted Dream Academy and had a hit single with 'Life In A Northern Town'. The remaining newcomers, among them a guard on the London Underground, eventually disappeared.

There was one presenter, however, that *The Tube* wanted but didn't get. 'We auditioned something like 500 people and everybody had five minutes to say why they should be a presenter,' said Andrea Wonfor. 'There was one guy who came along who was very weirdly dressed and he was brilliant. He was funny and

Boy George – the one that got away

witty. Fantastic.' The bizarrely dressed stranger was George O'Dowd – Boy George. Culture Club was just taking off and he turned down *The Tube* to concentrate on the band. 'He was in a wedding dress, the full thing,' said Malcolm Gerrie. 'I remember him leaving the audition in the pouring rain and jumping into a black cab with his dress trailing in the road as it pulled away.'

Channel 4 was just three days old when *The Tube* went on air. Chief Executive Jeremy Isaacs had felt that a live music show was a vital building block in the channel's schedule. In the Sixties, while working for Rediffusion TV, he had witnessed first-hand the atmosphere generated by *Ready, Steady, Go!*, which was broadcast live each week.

Friday evenings in those days saw him leaving his office at Television House in London's West End and having to negotiate the crowds queuing to get into the basement studio of the building. It was a memory that stayed with him as he began to shape Channel 4.

In *The Tube* he was looking for a show which would have its own personality yet somehow recreate some of the spirit of *Ready, Steady, Go!*: 'I was absolutely clear it should be live and in the early part of the evening,' he said. 'I also believed that programmes should be as long as they could be. And I felt the weekend would start with *The Tube*.'

There was the latitude to experiment, not only in terms of the look of the show, but with content too. There was imaginative use of black and white archive footage. Artists and sculptors appeared. There was just as likely to be a feature on 3-D television as an item on crafting cheap furniture out of cardboard boxes. A rich vein of comedy ran throughout the shows. Mark Miwurdz, a satirical poet from Sheffield, had a regular stand-up spot. Always there were the bands. 'The thing about *The Tube* is it wasn't just a music programme,' said former producer Paul Corley. 'There were lots of feature items and films. It was a concert with a kind of build-up. Suddenly – bang – you were into live bands at the end.'

'It was healthy because there were lots of creative people and they would just make it up as they went along,' said Jools. 'One person would be working for weeks on head lice or something and one person would be wanting to film in New York, and there would be all these things going on. It was a rather good, mad mix and there was lots of spontaneity.'

If there were any rules it was hard to know what they were. While other programmes were bound by rigid formats *The Tube* pleased itself. 'We were able to bend all the rules of TV,' said Paul Corley. 'But we had to know the rule book in order to vary it. Anyone who thought *The Tube* was thrown together knew nothing about television.'

Corley was an experienced producer with extensive knowledge of live programming. Before moving to Newcastle he had spent 18 months on the BBC magazine show, *Nationwide*. 'It was quite a change from Frank Bough and Sue Lawley to Jools and Paula,' he said. Behind the scenes the production team worked tirelessly to get the right mix of music on the show. They listened to every demo tape that came into the building. They went to endless gigs. Every Monday morning there was a meeting at which researchers would fight for their favoured bands. Frequently there were furious exchanges. Ultimately, the line-up for each show was down to Malcolm Gerrie. From the outset he was keen for *The Tube* to set its own agenda without feeling unduly influenced by record companies or the music press. An essential element of that agenda was the quest to feature new talent whenever possible.

Inevitably, the experimental nature of the show threw up the occasional band or feature that just didn't work. One of the films featured in the first *Tube* was shot in Birmingham with a dance company called Danse d'Afrique. Owing to an unfortunate slip, they appeared on the official posters as Dance To Freak. 'It was terminally arty and boring and we thought: "Never again,"' said Andrea Wonfor. 'There were some bloody awful items, dreadful ones,' recalled Chris Cowey. 'Lots of little interviews we used to have in the foyer of Studio 5, Jools talking to the editor of *Jamming* magazine, and all these kids who'd presumably been dragged off the streets because they were mods. Now it's unwatchable. There was an awful lot of crap, but what everyone remembers is The Jam.'

Midway through the first series a rap duo called Laurel And Hardy opened the show with a song called 'Clunk Click'. Dry ice swirled across the studio floor as a couple of models in an open-topped sports car fastened and released their seat belts in time to the music. 'That brings back horrible memories,' said Chris Cowey. 'A couple of guys doing this dodgy pseudo-reggae rap with the message clunk click every trip, was just so appallingly awful. How that got through...'

Former researcher Chris Phipps remembers a band called Michaelangelo's David, filmed during one of *The Tube*'s early shoots in Birmingham. Dressed in togas they recited a soliloquy from *Hamlet*. 'I just thought: "What the hell is that?" Maybe we were trying to be worthy or something.'

When things went wrong, or there was a particularly turgid item, no one really cared. Much of *The Tube*'s charm lay in the fact it was rough around the edges. What one critic called, 'cheerfully amateurish'.

Just a few weeks into the first series, the *Sun*'s Margaret Forwood wrote a scathing review. 'The pop show which seems to have been thrown together by some of the unemployed teenagers so much of Channel 4 is aimed at,' she said.

Jeremy Isaacs was unperturbed. 'If it was rough, I liked that. I didn't want everything to be smooth and warm with everything that had gone wrong edited out. I liked the idea of a live event,' he said. 'I believed it was of the absolute essence that we should take risks. We were told to be a distinctive service, to encourage innovation in the form and content of programmes, and that is the precise phrase that justifies for me *The Tube*.'

Not all critics disliked the rawness of the show. 'If it's inept at least it's honest,' wrote Frances Farrer in *The Times Educational Supplement*.

'Because it had such a lot going for it people forgave *The Tube* its faults,' said Andrea Wonfor. 'It's like watching football – if you're a fan you'll go and watch Newcastle United every week and you'll watch a goalless draw two weeks running because you know there's going to be some excitement. We set ourselves the task that the show would have a couple of what we used to call fuck-off moments. Real magic moments.'

A rap duo called Laurel And Hardy opened the show with a song called 'Clunk Click'. Dry ice swirled across the studio floor as a couple of models in an open-topped sports car fastened and released their seat belts in time to the music. 'That brings back horrible memories.'

One of those moments comprised the Weather Girls singing 'It's Raining Men' while in a corner of the studio a muscular individual blew up hot water bottles until they burst.

'It just worked. It was the challenge of being inventive and that sense of "What am I seeing?"' said Andrea Wonfor.

Whatever its faults and foibles, *The Tube* was genuine. Everyone who worked on the show shared a real passion for music and a desire to create something original. It may have been rough, but it consistently broke new ground. Jools, reflecting on it all, said, 'It wasn't contrived, that was the main thing about it. It genuinely was just a bit shoddy.' Paula agreed. 'It genuinely was good when it was good, but that was just by chance.'

For the million or so viewers who watched *The Tube* it was a refreshing antidote to the more established music shows of the time, like *Top Of The Pops* and *The Old Grey Whistle Test*. '*Top Of The Pops* had become a painting-by-numbers light entertainment show with lots of flashing lights and very little coolness or credibility,' said Chris Cowey. 'You had to have street cred – and *The Tube* had a complete obsession with credibility.'

When Channel 4 announced it had commissioned a live music show from Tyne Tees, there were mutterings about whether Newcastle could ever command the same credibility as London. Commissioning Editor Mike Bolland remembers the reaction to the news at a press conference in the Theatre Royal in Drury Lane. Elkan Allen, a former producer of *Ready, Steady, Go!,* was present and voiced his disapproval. 'He said we were crazy, that the only place to do it from was the West End of London,' said Mike Bolland. 'There was nothing more satisfying for me when not only were bands prepared to go to Newcastle, but they were also prepared to play live.'

There were, in fact, sound reasons behind the decision to commission Tyne Tees to make the series. The company had a long tradition of entertainment specials and an outstanding track record for music and youth programming. 'We already had a team together doing hit shows and trying to make them look different,' said Andrea Wonfor. Integral to that team was Malcolm Gerrie, a former English teacher from Sunderland, who came to Tyne Tees on a six-month contract to work on a show called *Glamour Trail*. It was his passion for music that made him the obvious candidate to develop the regional rock show, *Alright Now*, regarded by many as the forerunner of *The Tube*.

Gerrie was insistent that bands play live. He experimented with guest presenters, using talent as diverse as Billy Connolly and Mickey Most. And he made a point of featuring unknown bands. Among those given an early break on *Alright Now* were The Police and Dire Straits. 'It was not as if we'd never done anything like it before,' said Gavin Taylor, who directed *Alright Now*. 'We knew how to cope with live music.'

This experience made them clear favourites to produce Channel 4's new flagship music show. Mike Bolland was familiar with the work of Andrea Wonfor and Malcolm Gerrie and felt they were better placed than anyone to produce a successful Eighties version of *Ready, Steady, Go!*. An added bonus was that Jeremy Isaacs had worked with Tyne Tees director of programmes Andy Allen, and had absolute faith in his abilities. 'His was the best judgment of popular taste in a certain kind of programming of anyone I'd ever known or worked with,' he said.

Andrea Wonfor and her team submitted their proposal for a series of six pre-recorded programmes called *Jamming*. The hour-long format mixed music and comedy with magazine elements. It was not what Channel 4 had in mind. Mike Bolland's response was to ask if they could do a live show. Andrea Wonfor said they could. How about an hour and forty-five minutes? 'I just said, "What?" The slot was so exciting. Suddenly we had much more time to play around in, and all our old ideas about programme

formats went out the window,' she said. There was one more stipulation from Channel 4. They wanted 20 shows. 'We didn't muck about,' said Jeremy Isaacs. 'Make it long and keep it live, and let's see how we go.'

Malcolm Gerrie was in Sweden filming a special with Abba for another Tyne Tees show *Razzmatazz* when the news came through. 'As soon as Andrea told me they didn't want *Jamming* I hit the roof,' said Gerrie. 'I was ranting and raving and she was just saying – listen. Finally she managed to get a word in edgeways to say they wanted 20 shows. It was unbelievable.'

Locating the show in Newcastle, 300 miles away from the heart of the music industry, was a gamble which paid off for Channel 4. Without question, the character of *The Tube* owed much to its north-east roots. 'What happens with a lot of television made in London is that you're much more conscious of what people think of you,' said Andrea Wonfor. 'Up there it was Geordies versus the rest. We never ever thought about what it should be seen to be, or what constituencies we should aim to please. We wanted to make something wholly original. I think it had a lot of bollocks, which it wouldn't have had if it had come out of London. The core thinking was very Geordie.'

From the outset the physical distance from the capital worked to the advantage of the show. 'Because we were away from all the hype you get in London and the commercial pressures and the record companies and the press living on your doorstep, and because it was Newcastle – unfashionable backwater that everyone

assumes it is – we were left to get on with it,' said Chris Cowey. 'We were insulated from all the bullshit, and to a large extent insulated from the pressure. We were like kids in a candy store.'

There was also something about Newcastle itself – a quality peculiar to the city – which contributed to *The Tube*'s unique style. 'I think the physical structure of the place, the extraordinary changes of level that you encounter if you try to walk round it, are very exciting,' said Jeremy Isaacs. 'It's a city that appeals to the eye in a very remarkable way. There's something about the bridges. I wouldn't be surprised if the notion of a camera that can do that –' he made a sweeping motion with his arm '– could be related to the Newcastle landscape.'

Satirical poet Mark Miwurdz. *The Tube* mixed comedy with music from the outset

Two:
New Discoveries

'There were endless people we filmed who you never heard of again but it didn't matter.'

Jools Holland

IT WAS ON A COLD AND DREARY SUMMER'S DAY in 1982 that 30,000 fans packed into Gateshead International Stadium for a special *Tube* event. The Police topped a bill that featured Lords Of The New Church, Gang Of Four, The Beat and U2.

Director Gavin Taylor vividly remembers the day. He had been on holiday in France and was flown back for the event. *The Tube* was due to air a few months later and this was to be the first rock concert he would direct. 'It was all new to me,' he said. 'I didn't know U2 but their performance was absolutely electric. I remember Bono climbing the scaffolding on the stage at one point, going right to the top, and singing from up there. It was very hairy to watch.'

It was the Gateshead Stadium concert that marked the beginning of *The Tube*'s long-running relationship with U2. 'It seemed to me we played *The Tube* many, many times,' said the band's manager Paul McGuinness. 'It almost became like a residency.'

When *The Tube* went on air in the autumn of 1982 U2 were still looking for their big break. The not-too-distant past had seen them playing small venues to a handful of people. Jools remembers Squeeze and U2 doing a gig together at the Hope And Anchor in London. 'There were just three people there,' he said.

All that was about to change and *The Tube* was to play its part. There was something about the energy of the show that appealed to the band. Playing *The Tube* always felt more like a gig than a television programme. 'They had a very good crew,' said Paul McGuinness. 'I think Gavin Taylor must have been the key to it creatively. They were very rock 'n' roll roadie types from Newcastle with a very band-friendly attitude.

U2's appearance way down the bill at a *Tube* concert at Gateshead International Stadium in 1982 marked the beginning of their close relationship with the show

Doing *Top Of The Pops* at that time was a miserable experience – all these BBC lifetime employees telling you where to stand. It was very relaxed on *The Tube*.'

A lasting friendship developed between the band and *Tube* producer Malcolm Gerrie. In a recent interview Bono, reflecting on his career, identified three significant influences. Gerrie was among them. 'Two things broke U2 and one of them was *The Tube*,' said Paul McGuinness. The other was playing four consecutive Monday nights at the Marquee, then in London's Wardour Street.

When the band decided to plough the profits from their album *War* into a concert at the open-air Red Rocks venue in Denver, Colorado, in 1983, it was obvious who would film it. *Tube* producer Malcolm Gerrie and director Gavin Taylor were drafted in. 'They had a way of filming music that was very exciting,' recalled bass player Adam Clayton. 'We probably felt a great deal of trust and confidence that they were able to work in a guerrilla-like fashion.'

Red Rocks, an old Indian burial ground high above Denver, was a dramatic setting for a concert. 'What was good primarily about Red Rocks was that it was not humungous,' said Adam Clayton. 'It comes across on camera as being very big but I think it had a capacity of about 6,000. An outdoor gig at a mountain location with all those rock formations was going to look good. The power of that was important.'

Despite the natural beauty of the location, Gavin Taylor felt there was scope for improvements that would work to the band's advantage. 'I felt we had to build a rock 'n' roll stage and that there had to be a close connection between the band and the audience,' he said. Hence the runway from the stage out into the crowd. Paul McGuinness, meanwhile, brought in special effects specialists from Los Angeles to install propane fires all around the amphitheatre. 'There was barely time to catch breath,' said Gavin Taylor. 'As soon as we arrived in Denver we were straight into meetings, then off to take a look at the location. Then we had to start getting it built.'

American technicians and a local production company were drafted in to construct and rig. There were no rehearsals. On the day of the gig, however, the weather threatened to make a mockery of all the hard work and careful planning.

Black clouds had gathered over Denver and the city was experiencing its worst rains in living memory. At Red Rocks the stage was waterlogged. As the downpour continued an army of assistants made futile attempts to sweep pools of water off the stage. The concert – on which U2 were taking a huge financial gamble – was looking like a complete washout. 'It was very on again, off again,' said Adam Clayton. 'We sat in the hotel in the afternoon looking out of the window and talking constantly about a) whether the environment was surviving in the rain and b) whether it was safe to power up any equipment, considering how wet it was.'

As rumours circulated that the show was off, the band resolved to go ahead. Although some of the lighting equipment had been rendered useless by the downpour the music system was still working. 'We knew we could do a show and we had to shoot that day. We couldn't afford not to – if we hadn't gone ahead we'd have been walking home from Denver,' said Adam Clayton. 'It was very scary at the time because all our money was invested in it,' said Paul McGuinness.

Meanwhile, as conditions worsened, the support bands began to pull out. 'Barry Fay, the promoter, saw the electricity arc from one speaker column to another like lightning and said, "That's it." It was horrendous,' said Malcolm Gerrie.

U2. The Edge and Bono

The rain continued to fall throughout the day. On stage, waterproof sheets lay draped over equipment. Despite the torrential conditions the fans began arriving, many on foot, and all soaked to the skin. 'It was very touch and go,' said Gavin Taylor. 'I remember having very little sleep the night before and sitting backstage worrying. It was very nerve-wracking.' According to Malcolm Gerrie, 'The band had locked themselves in a room and I don't know what they did but they're quite religious and I'm sure they prayed. They had all their money, everything, locked up in the gig.'

Towards the end of the day the rain finally began to ease off. Pockets of mist hung in the air as it continued to drizzle. After hours of uncertainty U2 appeared on stage, playing to less than half the capacity of the venue. Incredibly, in the end, the deluge and its aftermath worked to the advantage of the band and production crew.

'It was amazing,' said Adam Clayton. 'A couple of miles up a mountain in an atmosphere that's so very special. A lot of things conspired to make it an event for the people who were there.' 'Because of the atmospheric conditions, which were really weird, everyone was steaming,' said Malcolm Gerrie. 'The camera lenses and the tungsten lamps and the moisture exaggerated the effect.'

Gavin Taylor remembers how the event took on a strange, almost spiritual quality. 'In a way I think it was meant to be. It gave the whole thing an unbelievable look – mist in the air, steam coming off Bono's body – I can't describe it. It was just amazing. No one could decide if it was a rock concert or some kind of religious gathering.' Once the concert was over there was a celebration dinner in Denver. The band had every reason to feel good. At the eleventh hour they had pulled off an amazing event – and averted financial disaster.

The subsequent video, *Under A Blood Red Sky*, was highly praised. One reviewer called it 'far and away the most exciting and memorable chunk of concert footage seen on video for a long time'. A bestseller on both sides of the Atlantic, it helped U2 establish their particular brand of music in the US. To date, around half a million copies of the video and three million albums have been sold. 'It was a hugely successful venture, but at the time we were rolling the dice,' said Paul McGuinness. 'At the time, British music was very synthesiser pop-orientated,' said Adam Clayton. 'We didn't fit into that format of pretty boys wearing make-up. In a way, Red Rocks allowed us to take a photograph of where we were coming from. Ours was a more guitar-led, confrontational sound and performance.'

Fresh from the triumph of Red Rocks Malcolm Gerrie and Gavin Taylor arrived back in Newcastle to find another storm brewing. *The Tube* had secured the rights to show the entire concert, but there was opposition from the technicians' unions at Tyne Tees. 'They felt we should have taken more people out to Denver,' said Gavin Taylor. 'After much negotiation and persuasion we reached an agreement to show 15 minutes of footage.'

The Red Rocks experience cemented the relationship between U2 and *The Tube*. A degree of mutual trust and respect had been established which would prove enduring. 'They were completely unspoiled,' recalled Gavin Taylor. 'I remember sitting with them in their hotel room chatting. We became good friends. I had a great

Frankie Goes To Hollywood – something for everyone

deal of respect for them. Their hearts were in the right place and they had no airs and graces.'

'Of all the people I've met in the industry U2 are singularly the best to work with,' said Malcolm Gerrie. 'They're constantly hungry to do new things and I think that's so exciting.'

When *The Tube* came to an end in April 1987, U2, on tour in the States, sent a farewell message to their old friends, recorded in their hotel room in San Diego. 'We've just heard the sad and the bad news that it's all over for the best rock 'n' roll show on TV, *The Tube*,' said Bono. 'If *The Tube* hadn't been behind us I think we would have found it a lot more difficult,' said Adam Clayton. 'I think they also became friends. It was part of a relationship between peers – people we respected and they respected us.'

The Tube was well into the stride of its first series when, in January 1983, a crew was dispatched to Liverpool to make a number of films, including one featuring local band Echo And The Bunnymen in concert. On the same shoot, in typical incongruous fashion, they filmed a land-speed record attempt through the Mersey Tunnel. They also discovered an unknown band called Frankie Goes To Hollywood, and set in motion an extraordinary success story.

It was researcher Mick Sawyer who first spotted the band playing at a pub in Liverpool. *The Tube* decided to film them in the grandiose setting of the city's State Ballroom, where they

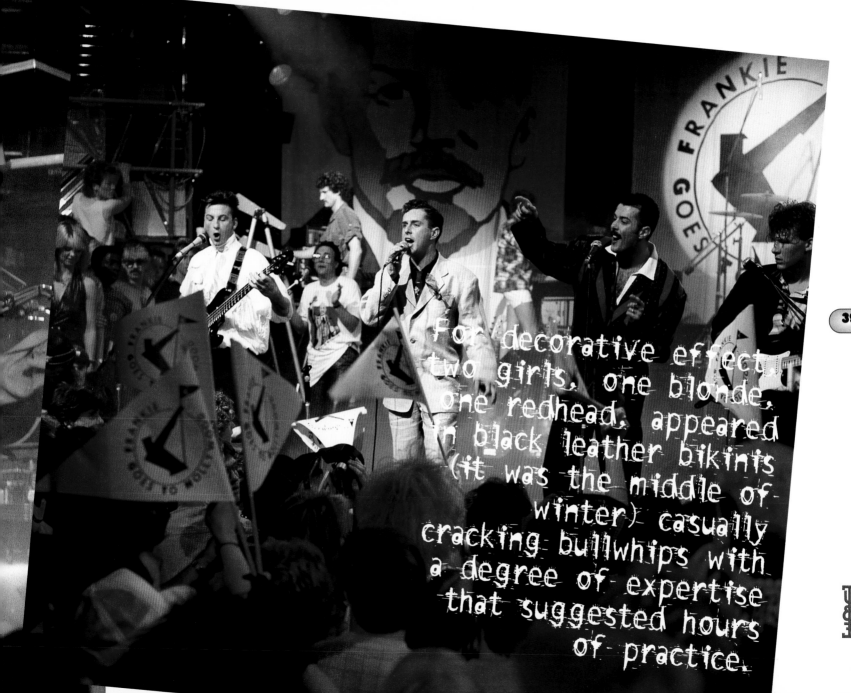

For decorative effect, two girls, one blonde, one redhead, appeared in black leather bikinis (it was the middle of winter) casually cracking bullwhips with a degree of expertise that suggested hours of practice.

rehearsed. They would perform a song called 'Relax (In Heaven Everything Is Fine)'.

On the day of the shoot, the band arrived at the location casually dressed in jeans and T-shirts. 'They appeared very low-key and down to Earth,' said one member of the production crew. After a morning of rehearsals and a lunch of takeaway pizzas, however, they disappeared to change into their stage gear. The crew watched with renewed interest as the band trooped back into the ballroom in bondage gear. Singer Holly Johnson sported skimpy red shorts, a cropped string vest and a leather cap. There was a profusion of black leather and dark glasses. For decorative effect two girls – one blonde, one redhead – appeared in black leather bikinis (it was the middle of winter) casually cracking bullwhips with a degree of expertise that suggested hours of practice. A pair of handcuffs dangled provocatively from the blonde girl's panties. These were the Leather Pets. 'I knew it was going to be a different kind of video when we started and one of the ladies sat on the lens,' said director Geoff Wonfor. 'I thought, "Oh dear." And it was rude. Very rude.' The film crew's production assistant, Michael Metcalf, who kept a diary, remembers the entry that day. 'Something for everybody. Two guys, two gays and two girls,' it read.

The director was in experimental mood. A few nights earlier he'd seen the movie *Jaws* at the cinema. One particular shot had intrigued him so much he saw the movie a second time to try and work out how it was done. 'There's that wonderful shot where the cop first sees the shark and the whole background wraps around itself. I thought, "How the fuck did he do that?"' said Geoff Wonfor. The trick was to track in on the subject and simultaneously zoom out at exactly the same speed.

Geoff Wonfor decided he would use the same technique to shoot the opening of the Frankie Goes To Hollywood film. Obligingly, the band extended the drum intro on

'Relax' so that there was time to achieve the Spielberg-inspired opening shot.

After four attempts the director was confident it was in the can. 'There was one elementary mistake,' says Geoff Wonfor. 'We didn't have anything up the sides as the camera moved in, so we didn't have any perspective, whereas in *Jaws* there were people all over the beach. When we got back I pissed myself. *One* lamp in the background had moved *one* foot. That was it. That was the effect. Didn't work at all.'

The film was striking enough anyway. Bizarrely, the State Ballroom, with its rococo ceilings and old-fashioned glamour, made an ideal setting for a thoroughly contemporary S&M band. That night the band went back to the crew's hotel for drinks. It was Jools's birthday, although he remembers little about it, despite a banner slung across the entrance of the Holiday Inn. HAPPY BIRTHDAY JOOLS, it said in big letters. That night there was a considerable amount of carousing. 'I think we had a very big knees-up. Mind you, we always did,' said Jools.

When the film appeared on *The Tube* a few weeks later it caught the eye of record producer Trevor Horn, who'd tuned in to the show at a recording studio in Willesden, where he was producing an album for the band Yes. 'They had these girls chained to the walls and I think the Frankies were wearing something called bum-splitters so the cheeks of their bottoms were naked, which was sort of odd. And codpieces and stuff like that,' he recalled. 'I was just bemused. I'd never seen anything like it. The whole thing looked kind of bizarre. They were naughty boys.'

A week or so later he heard 'Relax' again – this time during a Radio 1 session the band had recorded for David Jensen. The lyrics at once struck him as mildly pornographic. 'I thought, "My goodness, that song is so blatantly about sex." In a way it was very dirty, I think, but appealing. I thought, "That's a hit, that really is a hit song. I'm sure I could make that into a hit song.'"

Horn signed the band to ZTT Records and began re-working 'Relax', experimenting with four different recordings before arriving at the definitive version. The original middle eight which featured in *The Tube* film – 'In heaven everything is fine/you've got yours and I've got mine' – was dropped. Once the single was released, its lyrics got it banned by the BBC although, ironically, the corporation's real quarrel was nothing to do with the song itself.

Paul Morley of ZTT had featured a line – which never actually appeared in the song – on the record sleeve. 'The actual line was "Relax, don't do it, when you want to sock it to it,"' said Trevor Horn. 'Paul Morley had written, "when you want to suck it do it." That's what got it banned.' The week the BBC announced its ban *The Tube* played the video and invited Holly Johnson into the studio.

'*The Tube* was fantastic,' said Trevor Horn. 'I loved their whole attitude. When a show goes out live it gives it something that it never has when it's recorded.

Paul Young made his first TV appearance on *The Tube* in February 1983

You never quite knew if it was going to work. Sometimes it worked brilliantly, sometimes it didn't. But it was a good format. Full of energy.'

'Relax' topped the UK charts for five weeks, selling more than two million copies. 'I still think it was the greatest produced record of the decade. Fantastic,' said Geoff Wonfor, who counts the original demo among his most prized possessions. 'I suppose that was one element of *The Tube*,' said Jools. 'We got to people first and also gave people a break.'

'The one thing they did promise me, if they're reading this, was a black BMW when they made their first million,' said Geoff Wonfor. 'And I'm still fucking waiting.'

The Frankies went on to play live in Studio 5, minus bum-splitters, and without the Leather Pets. There was still a whiff of erotica in the air, however, thanks to a lady who slithered around in a state of undress on a nearby stage. As for the original girls, sisters Julie and Marie Muscatelli, they went on to do secretarial courses at Kirby College in Liverpool and announced plans for a solo career. They played at least one gig subsequently – a church carol service with their college choir in 1985 – for which leather bikinis were not suitable attire. 'It should be said that there were endless people we filmed who you never heard of again, but it didn't really matter,' said Jools. 'We gave them all the same care and attention and that was one of the good things which separated *The Tube* from programmes that had gone before.'

Around the same time as *The Tube* encountered Frankie Goes To Hollywood, another aspiring artist came to the notice of the show. This time it was *The Tube*'s stage manager Colin Rowell and associate producer Jeff Brown who spotted Paul Young playing at The Venue in London's Victoria. 'We'd gone down to see Grandmaster Flash,' said Colin Rowell. 'They were booked to appear on *The Tube* and it was the early days of turntable mixing, so we went to have a look and see what they were going to need.' Paul Young was the support act. Colin Rowell remembers the hairs standing up on the back of his neck as he watched him perform.

'I was captivated by him. I thought he was wonderful,' he said. He returned to Newcastle enthusing about the singer. At the time The Venue was being run by Ged Doherty, who was also managing Paul Young.

He had first encountered the singer while working as a junior booker for a London agency. At the time Paul Young was singing with a band called Streetband, who'd had a one-off hit with 'Toast' before going their separate ways. A few months later Ged Doherty made the transition from agent to manager and began representing the artist. By 1981 the singer was pursuing a solo career as well as playing with his band

The Q-Tips. In November of that year CBS signed him up. His two roles continued to develop in parallel. 'I remember one gig supporting Tom Petty And The Heartbreakers in Coventry as Paul Young and after we got offstage jumping in the van and driving up to Sheffield to play as The Q-Tips two hours later,' said Ged Doherty. 'It was an interesting time. We were young and stupid and excited by everything and it was great.'

It was in February 1983 that Paul Young was booked to appear on *The Tube*. 'That was the first break we had for Paul,' said Ged Doherty. 'All we knew was this was our first TV and I always knew if I could get Paul on TV, if people could see him live, that we were onto a winner.' Paul Young's appearance on the show coincided with a spoof celebration of the space race. 'Today is Buzz Aldrin's sister-in-law's birthday,' Jools announced from the roof of Tyne Tees as a computer-generated flying saucer scudded across the night sky.

It was a typically eclectic show. There was an interview with actor William Shatner – alias Captain Kirk of *Star Trek* – filmed on the set of his new TV series, *TJ Hooker*, in Los Angeles. Live in the studio were Aztec Camera and The Gap Band. Pop promoter Paul Loasby gave details of an Orwellian festival to usher in 1984 – tickets priced, appropriately, at 19.84. (In between arranging New Year parties he went on to become Jools Holland's agent.) 'It was definitely mad,' recalled Paul Young. 'I mean, the whole thing was crazy.'

He performed three numbers – 'Love Will Tear Us Apart', 'Love Of The Common People' and 'Sex' – and caused a minor sensation with his bra-less backing singers, The Fabulous Wealthy Tarts. 'Everybody was incredibly excited,' said Ged Doherty. 'Afterwards, there was a phenomenal response and everyone was getting drunk. We went back to the hotel and heard later that night they wanted us on again

Roland Gift – nerves got
the better of him prior
to a *Tube* shoot

the following week, so everybody got even drunker.'

Appropriately, it was Colin Rowell and producer Malcolm Gerrie who went to the singer's hotel to ask him back a second time. Paul Young was the first artist to play live on two consecutive shows. 'People thought that Paul was incredible – great performer, great voice, he looked great,' said Ged Doherty. 'And they were blown away with all the different elements of the band. They could really play, and the girls were really visual.'

'Getting that first appearance on *The Tube* was a very credible way of breaking through because the whole thing was live and you really had to prove yourself,' said Paul Young. 'There's a vibe you get that's so different to miming. It's a much better atmosphere when you've got great bands on and they're doing their thing with no real restrictions. They just go out and do a good performance and you've got a really great atmosphere, which is very difficult to do on TV actually. But *The Tube*

managed to get it week by week.'

The first time Paul Young appeared on *The Tube* he did the journey to Newcastle in the old Transit van he toured in. He and the band stayed in a shabby hotel and spent two nights on the town partying at Julie's nightclub in relative obscurity. 'It was interesting going up to Newcastle that first week when Paul was relatively unknown,' said Ged Doherty. 'Going back the following week it was as if the whole city suddenly knew him. It was quite incredible the effect the show had. You could tell just from the number of girls hanging round.' *The Tube* marked a dramatic turning point for the singer. All of a sudden his career took off.

Fine Young Cannibals adopted the *Tube* film as their official video for 'Johnny Come Home'

'That appearance on *The Tube* changed people's perceptions overnight,' said Ged Doherty. 'Suddenly people were talking about Paul. In terms of his status with the record company, it instantly had a huge effect. I had no idea the impact would be so long-lasting. For years afterwards people were still saying they remembered the first time they'd seen Paul on *The Tube*. It was quite phenomenal.'

Fine Young Cannibals were another *Tube* success story. When The Beat broke up in

1983 guitarist Andy Cox and bass player Dave Steele decided to form a new band. Vocalist Roland Gift completed the line-up.

In the summer of 1984 a demo tape arrived in *The Tube* office. The song was 'Johnny Come Home'. 'It sounded like Van Morrison mixed with Otis Redding,' said former researcher Chris Phipps.

He was soon on his way to Birmingham to see the band – then unsigned – in a bare studio. 'They were very charismatic,' he said. 'There was an extraordinary quality to Roland Gift's voice, lots of dynamics in their music. It was very simple in a way, very stripped-down, and at the same time very original.'

In early 1985 *The Tube* returned to the same studio and filmed Fine Young Cannibals performing 'Johnny Come Home'. Director Geoff Wonfor remembers Roland Gift suffering an attack of nerves prior to the shoot. A production assistant was sent off to find a medicinal bottle of brandy and the singer downed three large measures before filming got underway. 'We'd actually been on a ten-day shoot and that was the last thing we were doing,' said Geoff Wonfor. 'We had a train to catch and I was dog-tired. I did four takes and that was it, thank you very much, and we were off. It took between $13\frac{1}{2}$ and 15 minutes.'

Within a matter of weeks the film – adopted as the video for the single – was on MTV, and Fine Young Cannibals were on their way to a top ten hit. Roland Gift and Geoff Wonfor have been friends ever since.

The Housemartins came to the attention of *The Tube* through Andy McDonald, who ran an independent label called Go! Discs. The band had been touring as the support act to one of the record

(Opposite) Billy Bragg became a familiar face on the show. (Below) The Housemartins – a low-key gig in Peterborough led to an appearance on *The Tube*

48

company's other artists, Billy Bragg, and came highly recommended. 'I went to see them play in the downstairs bar of a pub called the Clarendon on Hammersmith Broadway,' said Andy McDonald. 'I thought Paul Heaton was an amazing front man – a fantastic, soulful singer. And lyrically they were so good. When you have artists making music around really good songs and good singers you've got two vital components.'

He signed them and a few months later sent a tape of songs to *The Tube*. 'The band were due to play at this little community centre in Peterborough and *The Tube* sent along a guy called Chris Phipps to see them.' At that time The Housemartins, who played under a banner which read 'We're preaching the left-wing gospel', were attracting some unwanted attention from skinheads and other right-wing groups.

On the night of the Peterborough gig in the summer of 1985 only around forty people had turned out to see them. Andy McDonald suspected there might be trouble. 'As we were approaching the gig we could see all these silhouettes of nine-foot skinheads with knee-length Doc Martens. It was like, "What's going to happen here?"'

The band condensed their usual 50-minute set into just 37 minutes. 'It was a case of "Let's get it over as quickly as possible," but they played really well and went down well with the crowd.'

Even the skinheads were impressed. The threatened trouble failed to materialise. 'They played in that near-empty community centre as if they were performing before a capacity audience,' said Chris Phipps. 'They were extremely good, very fresh.'

The Tube decided to book the band, but rather than a live studio appearance they decided to film them in their battered old tour van.

The Proclaimers made it onto the show after sending in a video of 'Letter From America'

'They did it in a fantastic way,' said Andy McDonald. 'They really got into the culture of the band. And the band loved it, because it accurately reflected what they were about at the time. 'They were very generous in terms of what the band wanted to put into the film as well. Very open to suggestions, which was great.' Andy McDonald came to know *The Tube* well, through his association with both Billy Bragg and The Housemartins. 'We used to really enjoy being up there. It was typical Geordie hospitality – you'd end up in some hotel bar until three in the morning dancing to Motown tunes. It was never a case of being shunted off into a hotel and left.'

What struck him about the production team was their passion for music and their ability to spot emerging talent. 'They used to get it right. Some of the films they made around the bands were really imaginative. And they had very good instincts about the good bands that were coming through, like Fine Young Cannibals. You'd often find, as a record company, that the bands you were looking at were just about to go and do *The Tube*.'

A little over a year after making their debut on *The Tube* the Housemartins' first album *London o Hull 4* went gold, with sales topping 250,000 within a few months of its release. Their *a cappella* single 'Caravan Of Love', which premiered on *The Tube* in November 1986, went on to give them a UK number 1. 'The atmosphere on *The Tube* was always electric,' said Andy McDonald. 'It was organised chaos, a lot of frantic activity, people running round corridors. I know they got into trouble a few times but it was always really edgy.'

Around the same time a tape landed on the desk of Chris Phipps from a band called The Proclaimers, who'd supported The Housemartins on their 1986 tour. Twins Craig and Charlie Reid were looking for a spot on *The Tube*. The tape was promising but the duo were miles away in Aberdeen. 'I asked if they could find someone local who could make a video for them so we could see what they looked like,' said Chris Phipps. 'What arrived was a video of the guys walking round a fish quay singing 'Letter From America', badly out of sync. But they looked unusual and it was a great song so we booked them.' In January 1987 The Proclaimers played live on *The Tube*. 'Letter From America' became a big hit for them.

Chris Phipps proved an astute talent spotter. One of his more spectacular finds was the US heavy metal band Twisted Sister. He'd seen them play in New York a year before *The Tube* launched and was convinced they were destined for major success. 'They had elements of Alice Cooper and were a very clever mishmash of glam and metal and music hall,' he recalled. 'Dee Snider was an extraordinary singer. I'd never seen anything like them.'

Not everyone on the production team was a fan of heavy metal and Phipps remembers having to fight his corner to secure a spot for Twisted Sister. 'There was a constant battle between heavy metal and rock. Heavy metal wasn't considered hip. I can remember banging the table to get my own way.' Another of the

Twisted Sister with special guest Lemmy from Motorhead. A record deal followed their appearance on *The Tube*

Manchester's pride and joy – The Smiths

researchers, Chris Cowey, recalls weekly production meetings that lasted several hours as individuals fought for the bands they believed in. 'We were all very keen, very passionate, and we used to have serious arguments. There was lots of table-banging and people vying with each other to get their bands on.'

So keen was Twisted Sister to appear on *The Tube* that the band paid for their own flights from the US. It turned out to be a shrewd investment. On the day they arrived at Tyne Tees they caused mild consternation. A van pulled up outside the studios and five enormous guys with shoulder-length hair emerged. They looked like a bunch of mean, muscular bikers. As they sound-checked the studio mysteriously cleared. 'They looked pretty amazing. I think people were frightened of them,' said Chris Phipps. In fact, they were well-behaved at all times. In between rehearsals Mark 'The Animal' Mendoza buried himself in a copy of the *Sunday Times*.

When they performed Dee Snider – known for his liberal use of profanities – announced they'd cleaned up their act for *The Tube*: 'We've been told not to curse and *The Tube* people have been so nice to us we're not going to do any cursing.' They closed the show with a raucous 25-minute set. Lemmy and Brian Robertson from Motorhead, who'd guested on the same show, joined them for the last number to bring the house down.

Another guest on the show was Mick Jones of Foreigner, who'd arrived in Newcastle on a private jet accompanied by Phil Carson of Atlantic Records. Carson was so impressed he signed up Twisted Sister immediately and saw their album, *Stay Hungry*, go platinum. 'No programme since *The Tube* has given such a chance to unsigned bands,' said Chris Phipps.

Madonna already had a record deal but was relatively unknown when she made her first British TV appearance on *The Tube* in January 1984. She was booked for a live outside broadcast the show was doing from The Hacienda club in Manchester. Also appearing were the Factory All-Stars, Marcel, *Coronation Street*'s Pat Phoenix, drag queen Foufou Lamarr and Morrissey of The Smiths. Madonna was way down the bill. Producer Paul Corley recalls how Bill Fowler of WEA Records pushed for the artist to be booked. 'He swore this woman was going to be the biggest thing in pop.' Bill Fowler's faith in his act was interpreted as well-intentioned hype. All the same, it made sense to book Madonna for The Hacienda. The venue was exactly right for a disco routine.

On the day of the show, Madonna travelled to Manchester by train with two dancers.

Jools with Leslie
Ash, who took over
from Paula for the
second series.
'Presenting wasn't
her natural métier'

The moment she arrived at the club for rehearsals she appeared to have second thoughts. 'I remember her walking in,' said Chris Cowey, the researcher at the time. 'There was no management, no record company, no entourage, no nothing. She looked around and said: "What the fuck am I doing here?"' Since the Factory All-Stars were set up on the only stage, Madonna was relegated to the dancefloor. She rehearsed miming to a backing track and everything was set. 'It was actually a bit shambolic on the day,' said Chris Cowey. Shortly before going on air a generator went down. At the entrance to The Hacienda a couple of fire-eaters exhaled flames while impatient punters jostled to be let in. A frantic member of the production team, battling to maintain some semblance of order, ran up and down shouting 'Get back! You'll all be burned to death!'

Despite mild pandemonium, the show opened without a hitch as Jools, dodging fire-eaters, promised 'the most hectic *Tube* ever'. Like every *Tube* it had its moments. Guest presenter Tony Fletcher struggled through an interview with Morrissey without the benefit of studio talkback. It was clear communications had disintegrated. 'Currently one of the hottest bands in the country are Manchester's pride and joy, The Smiths,' he said before stopping abruptly. A moment of silence followed during which both Morrissey and Fletcher appeared thoroughly bemused. 'What's happening?' he said, glancing over his shoulder. What was happening was that he was live on air. Several seconds went by before he repeated the entire link.

It was during this interview that Morrissey made a memorable prediction when asked why there was no video to go with The Smiths' new single. 'We really want to bypass the whole video market,' he said. 'I think that's something that's going to die very quickly and I want to herald the death of that. I think it has nothing whatsoever to do with music.'

Two hundred miles away in Newcastle a tea dance was underway in the foyer at Tyne Tees. Lots of sailors in full uniform waltzed in the background as Leslie Ash introduced JB's All-Stars. Leslie had joined *The Tube* to present the second series after Paula – pregnant throughout the first – left to have Fifi.

Although a popular choice, Leslie never quite 'fitted' in the way Paula had. In essence, Leslie was an actress playing herself on the show, while Paula was never anything other than her inimitable self. 'It was a tough call for Leslie and presenting wasn't her natural métier,' said Malcolm Gerrie. 'As a learning curve it was vertical.' Leslie was adept enough but never as fearless or sassy as Paula. On the night of the Hacienda broadcast, however, she showed no sign of nerves as she carried the Newcastle end of the show single-handedly.

Back in Manchester, things continued to go awry for Tony Fletcher, who finally stomped off in exasperation as Tony Wilson of Factory Records and Paul Morley of rival ZTT engaged in a messy dispute over the merits of Manchester versus London. When the Factory All-Stars finally played the audience crowded onto the Hacienda's dancefloor.

By the time the area was cleared for Madonna it was a mess and there was no time to clean it up. 'There was beer spilt, bits of broken glass,' said Chris Cowey. 'People throwing fag ends and bits of pie at her. She was a complete trooper.'

Dressed in black from head to toe, her cropped top showing off her bare midriff, Madonna danced and mimed her way through two numbers, 'Burning Up' and 'Holiday'. Then, having earned the Musician's Union minimum of £200, she left. Back in Newcastle the production team watched Madonna's performance with a marked lack of enthusiasm. 'It was a pretty poor environment for her and I remember saying to Bill Fowler, So she's going to be the biggest thing in pop?' said Paul Corley.

'None of us knew what she was going to become,' said Chris Cowey. 'We didn't even mention her at the Monday meeting afterwards. Nobody said, "Wasn't she fantastic?" because all she'd done was a couple of good pop disco songs and danced to them.'

There was an altogether different vibe surrounding Terence Trent D'Arby when he made his first TV appearance on *The Tube* in early 1987. He came to the notice of the show when his management company sent in a demo tape. 'It was very much my kind of music,' said Chris Cowey, who subsequently went to London to see the singer play a showcase gig at Ronnie Scott's jazz club. 'I was absolutely blown away,' he said. 'The thing that stood out was his voice. It was like boiling chocolate.'

Immediately after the show, Chris Cowey was introduced to the singer. 'He went all glassy-eyed and said he really wanted his first television appearance to be *The Tube*.' Shortly afterwards Terence Trent D'Arby was on his way to Newcastle to perform two tracks – 'Wishing Well' and 'If You Let Me Stay' – live on the show. 'He had this amazing voice and an arrogance that was more playful than intentional,' said Chris Cowey. The pair struck up a lasting friendship. 'He was very funny and hugely enthusiastic, and he just looked the business.' *The Tube* played 'If You Let Me Stay' repeatedly over subsequent weeks. When it was released as a single it reached the UK Top 10.

'We had this rule,' said Paula, who interviewed Terence. 'Anyone black and under 30 I did. Anyone black and over 70 Jools did. I remember Terence really well. He was on for four weeks running and we basically discovered him. It gave you that feeling that the show really could break acts.'

Three: Class Acts

'You'd walk into the Rose And Crown and there'd be Miles Davis chatting to Jools over a pint of Scotch.'

Malcolm Gerrie, producer

ANYONE WHO THOUGHT THE TUBE would struggle to persuade bands to trek north to Newcastle was mistaken. Many for whom London was home enjoyed getting out of the capital. There was an easy-going air about Newcastle that bands enjoyed. The fans gave them their space. When Simple Minds appeared on *The Tube*, Jim Kerr went over the road afterwards for a quiet pint. There were private parties at the Gosforth Park Hotel each week. Paul Young was spotted in the early hours of the morning singing along to soul classics at Julie's nightclub on the quayside. 'Basically, the reason *The Tube* was good was because it was broadcast from Newcastle, which is a great place,' said Trevor Horn. 'I think the fact that it took all the pop stars out of their normal environment and up to the frozen bleak wasteland of the north-east, back to some kind of absolute reality, must have helped it enormously.'

The journey itself became part of *The Tube* experience. For many of the bands the East Coast Mainline was their preferred route. 'Everyone involved would be on the same train and we would stay in Newcastle after the show and get to know everyone

After playing *The Tube*, Jim Kerr of Simple Minds went over the road for a quiet pint

else, then go back to London the next day with a big hangover,' said Paul McGuinness, manager of U2. 'I always liked King's Cross Station,' said Jools. 'It felt like you were going somewhere exciting. I used to look out and be excited by the vision of the sprawl of Stevenage, or going across the witch-infested country of Peterborough, or through the great industrial monuments of York. I used to feel I'd travelled Britain on that particular train, the Flying Scotsman, with its awful breakfasts.'

For Paula too the weekly trip to Newcastle remains one of her most vivid memories. 'We'd always take the train up and Jools would get into a fight with the ticket collector 'cos I'd never got a first-class ticket,' she said. 'Every single week Jools would pay the difference so we could sit in first class. He's such a toff.'

While some travelled by train, others preferred to fly. The regular Thursday influx of bands to Newcastle's modest airport was at times startling. On one memorable occasion the Eurythmics, PiL, Billy Bragg and Tina Turner all emerged from the same flight. Tina Turner had long

On one occasion The Eurythmics, PiL, Billy Bragg and Tina Turner all emerged from the same flight

been an established star by the time she appeared on *The Tube*. But few could have predicted the extent to which her appearance on the show would regenerate her career.

Researcher Chris Phipps recalls how, in 1983, on the advice of promoter Barry Marshall, Turner cancelled a gig in Stockholm in order to come to Newcastle and do a live set for *The Tube*. It was to prove a major turning point for her. She played a 45-minute set, only coming off-stage when technicians finally threatened to pull the plug. When she performed her new single, 'Let's Stay Together', Heaven 17 joined her on-stage to perform backing vocals. The band's association with the singer had started when they produced the British Electric Foundation album, which featured Tina's version of 'Ball Of Confusion'. Martyn Ware and Glenn Gregory went on to produce 'Let's Stay Together'.

'Tina Turner was the most charming person. She had been out of things for a while but her voice and her performance were mind-blowing,' said Paul Corley. 'Afterwards she came up and said: "Was that okay?" We were all gobsmacked that she could be humble enough to wonder about the strength of her performance.'

Subsequently, she went on to have a brilliant solo career, enjoying major success with the *Private Dancer* album and, in 1984, appearing in the film *Mad Max: Beyond the Thunderdome*. The theme from the movie, 'We Don't Need Another Hero', gave her another hit.

It was typical of *The Tube* that during its lifetime the mix of stars who played live on the show ranged from The Jam and Julian Cope to Duran Duran and Culture Club. From Iggy Pop and ZZ Top to Soft Cell and Shalamar. From Dr John to Elton John, and hundreds of others. 'You could tell who were the really great artists because there was much more of a vibe in the room,' said Jools. 'When Miles Davis was on there was a big hushed awe.'

**Bizarrely, Cliff Richard
appeared on the same
show as Killing Joke
(opposite)**

The same reverential hush had
also fallen over the studio in the
presence of Paul McCartney. And
again when Elton John played *The
Tube* in 1985. 'Miles Davis was very
slow and to have him on at half-
past five in the afternoon was quite
a lot to take in. He hardly said
anything, but he gave me a
drawing,' said Jools. 'I think that's
probably my fondest memory of the
whole series.'

'The great thing about *The Tube*
was the mix. You could have REM
and the Eurythmics playing live, an
interview with Madonna, the new
Elton John video, and a string
quartet playing in the foyer. There
were really no boundaries,' said
Paul Corley. A prime example of the
mix of the show was Cliff Richard
and Killing Joke playing live on the
same bill in 1985. It was Cliff

Richard's first appearance on live TV for 15 years – and he was booked at his own request.

Casually dressed in red jogging pants and t-shirt, he sat among the audience chatting to Paula. *The Tube*, he said, had broken barriers in terms of the sound it delivered. 'Being a recording artist, one wants to make it sound as close to the record as one can,' he said. 'So therefore I've come with my band and I feel confident that when we do it it's going to sound alright at home.' He appeared on stage to close the show, immaculately dressed in a style wholly unfamiliar to *The Tube*. His choice of wet-look pink suit, worn with silver tie and box-fresh trainers, prompted Paula to introduce him as, 'The man wearing the most extravagant suit ever seen on *The Tube*.' As he had predicted, the sound was excellent.

Not every artist left the studio happy, however. When Robert Plant appeared on *The Tube* he had a throat problem and demanded the right to veto any tracks he was

unhappy with. The former Led Zeppelin vocalist recorded an extended set and then went to view the tapes in the cutting room. 'It was an excellent set,' said Paul Corley, 'But he sat and watched it looking very grim. In the end he said none of the tracks could be used. It was my worst moment.' Despite entreaties from the producers and from Plant's manager he remained intransigent. So determined was he that the master tapes would be destroyed that he took them away with him. 'Of course, the story got out and what we didn't know was that someone in the audience had been taping it,' said Corley. 'The following Sunday there were bootleg tapes on sale in the market.'

It was rare for bands to turn down an opportunity to appear on *The Tube*. Even in its early days the influence wielded by the show among the record-buying public was widely acknowledged. *The Tube*'s audience may never have risen much above a million but it was a powerful million. These were the people who bought singles and albums on a regular basis. And it was a fact that whoever appeared on *The Tube* on a Friday evening could expect to see sales of their records rocket the following day.

Almost without exception, bands were prepared to make huge efforts to appear on *The Tube*. When Scritti Politti pulled out of one of the early shows due to illness the American band Shalamar were drafted in at short notice. They were touring in the UK and it was a huge palaver to get them onto *The Tube* without disrupting their schedule. Their journey was planned with military precision. Following a gig in Brighton

Shalamar went to extraordinary lengths to appear on *The Tube*

Paula and superstar
interviewee

John Lydon of PiL. 'Excuse me, Mr Rotten, would you mind just stopping?'

68

Iggy Pop – finally he
fell over and just lay
there singing

a coach whisked them to Gatwick where two chartered jets were standing by to take them to Newcastle. A fleet of cars took them to the City Road studios where they played three numbers, did a quick change and hurtled back to the airport. From there it was on by private jet to Bristol. By 11 p.m. they were on-stage in Chippenham.

One band who could not be persuaded to appear on *The Tube* was Half Man Half Biscuit, who were offered a spot on the show in January 1986 just as they were poised for major success. At that time the band's album was number 1 in the independent album charts. The timing could not have been better. In fact, for reasons beyond the production team's control, the timing could not have been worse.

Half Man Half Biscuit were fanatical supporters of Fourth Division Tranmere Rovers and declined *The Tube* because it clashed with a home game. Producer Malcolm Gerrie, himself a keen Sunderland supporter, was not without sympathy. He offered to provide a helicopter to get the band back to the Tranmere ground in time for the second half. It was not enough. Gerrie suggested procuring a video of the game. It was to no avail. Half Man Half Biscuit had not missed a home game for five years and weren't about to blot their perfect attendance record.

During its five-year run *The Tube* managed to secure just about every major artist in the world. Among those who remained elusive were Michael Jackson and the Artist Formerly Known As Prince. Researcher Chris Phipps recalls a meeting in the offices of CBS in LA with Jackson's manager, Frank Dileo. 'He was a squat man wearing a crushed gold lamé jumpsuit. He called me Phipps throughout the meeting,' he recalled. 'I'd taken a showreel of *The Tube* and asked him about Michael Jackson appearing. He leapt up and said, "Michael ain't doing another fucking thing." That was the beginning of him becoming totally unavailable.'

He met the Artist Formerly Known As Prince's manager at the Marquee Sunset Hotel in LA. 'I'll never forget it because Kiss were lounging round the swimming pool outside,' he said. 'There was mild interest but it came to nothing.' In the end it mattered little. There were plenty of other big names happy to grace Studio 5 each week, some more raucous than others. 'People like Stiv Bators from Lords Of The New Church and Iggy Pop – classic rock and rollers – would never really get to do any TV because no one would have them,' said Chris Cowey. 'We used to positively encourage those incendiary characters 'cos they fitted perfectly with what the programme was meant to be about.'

It was during the first series that Iggy Pop first played live on *The Tube*. A few hours

**Tina Turner's voice
and performance was
mind-blowing**

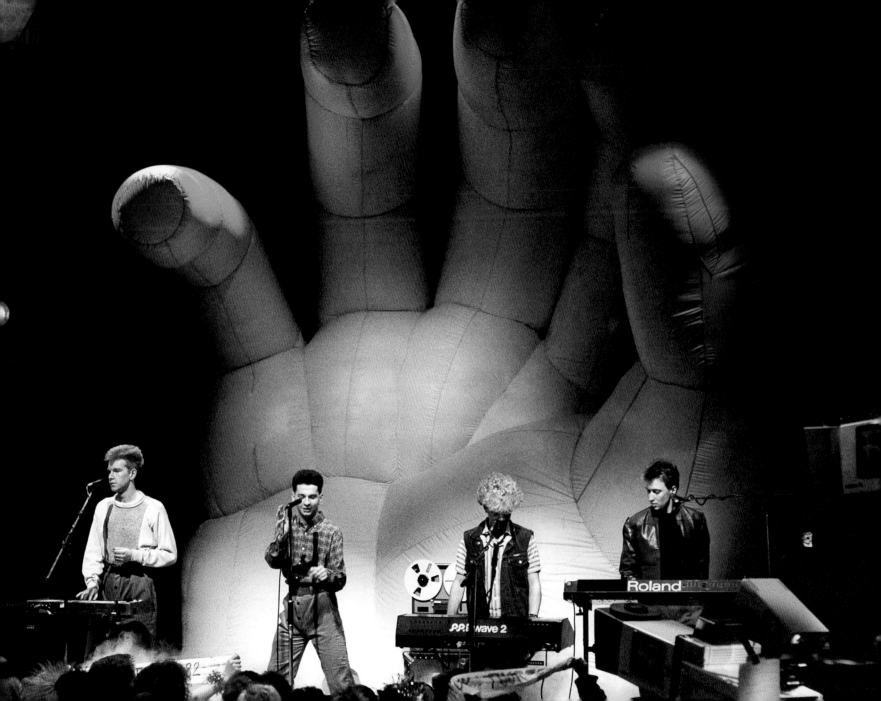

Tom Waits (and facing)
caught a bus back to his
hotel after the show

There were plenty of big
names happy to grace
Studio 5 each week.
Elton John played *The
Tube* in 1985

> '**We didn't pretend. We tried to be as truthful as possible.**'
>
> Geoff Wonfor, film director

Four: On the Road

IT WAS A BLISTERING HOT FEBRUARY MORNING in Kingston, Jamaica, and *The Tube* film crew was busy setting up for an interview with Gregory Isaacs. By midday the cameras were in place at the famous Zinc Fence Yard, an open-air venue. The crew, with director Geoff Wonfor, settled back to wait for the reggae singer to arrive. As they were about to discover, in Jamaica time is a fluid thing.

Several hours went by and numerous calls were made to Isaacs' record company. Despite repeated assurances he failed to appear. The crew, fortified by supplies of Red Stripe beer, settled in for a long wait in the baking heat. As darkness fell they began lighting the venue. More urgent calls to the record company followed. Gregory Isaacs was definitely on his way. Twelve hours later the director's patience was at breaking point. Finally, shortly after midnight, it snapped. He wrapped the unit and left. The following day it became clear why their man had stood them up.

'Gregory Isaacs wasn't even in the country,' said Geoff Wonfor. 'He didn't arrive until three days later.' 'He was in Glasgow doing a gig,' said producer Malcolm Gerrie. 'He was in America,' said Geoff Wonfor. 'I can't really remember the details,' said Jools. 'I experimented with the jazz cigarettes there and just had a very nice time.'

There were many such mishaps. On one occasion *The Tube* flew to the west coast of America to interview Stevie Wonder only to find that, due to a mix-up with his record company, he was 3,000 miles away on the east coast. 'I suppose I tended to get a bit more wound up then than I would now,' said Geoff Wonfor. 'Fortunately, I had a gaffer electrician called Ken Campbell who kept my head right during those difficult moments.'

For five years *The Tube* travelled the world making films that were innovative and original. One of their greatest strengths was that they were never hampered by preconceptions. While conventional wisdom dictated that film shoots should be carefully planned prior to arriving on location, *The Tube* preferred a more spontaneous approach. 'The mistake that lots of people in television make is that they take a view before they go and do the thing,' said Jools. 'We never did that. We'd go and look at people and say, "What do you want to do?" And then figure it out. So a lot of it came from the heart rather than from the head. I don't think you could do it these days. People get too fussed about their budgets and want to know exactly what's going to happen, whereas we just bowled up.'

The Tube was launched at the same time as pop videos were taking off. But while bands might have had hundreds of thousands of pounds to spend on a promotional video, *The Tube* was operating on a comparative shoestring. 'It's true that necessity is the mother of invention,' said director Geoff Wonfor. 'And I think we were very inventive.' Many of *The Tube* films were shot documentary style, using hand-held cameras. Often, they were starkly simple, always finely crafted.

Only *The Tube* could turn a simple telephone chat with George Michael into a work of art. 'George was away and all we could get was a phone interview,' said Paula. 'So we did it as a soft core porno thing with me in bed. It was a very simple thing, but it won lots of awards.' The resulting film was deemed so erotic it was sent for IBA approval

Wham! A phone interview with George Michael turned into a soft porn film

prior to being screened. 'It was very beautiful, but dodgy for then,' said Paula. 'I remember it well because there was trouble about it.'

At times, there were wonderfully elaborate sequences, which occasionally went hilariously wrong. The inspiration for a film with Dr Robert was the classic British movie *Brief Encounter*. 'That was my favourite film at the time,' said Paula. 'The amazing thing about *The Tube* was if you had a favourite movie Geoff would recreate it so you could be in it. Paula Yates suddenly stars in *Brief Encounter*!'

The location was an old station with a working steam train. In a departure from the usual hand-held style, the camera was to roll the entire length of the station in one smooth transition on a track which had been specially constructed, and stretched around 150 feet. It took several hours to set up for the shot, not least because getting the train in and out of the station was a tortuous procedure. 'It was absolutely perfectly done,' said Paula. 'It was so pretty and just exactly like the opening sequence of the movie.'

Finally, with everything in place, the train pulled into the station.

Geoff Wonfor remembers exactly what happened next. 'Harry Enfield's behind the counter in the café dressed as the serving lady, it's taken three hours to set it all up, and Paula's line is, "Have you got a glass of water? I've got something in my eye", which is the line from *Brief Encounter*. Dr Robert then says, "I'm a doctor, can I help you?" But Paula goes in and says, "Have you got a glass of water? I'm dying for a drink." I just said, "You're not dying for a drink – you've got something in your fucking eye!" Well she just turned and ran. She didn't stop for about 120 yards. Back we go to the fucking train. Another fucking two hours later...' Eight hours and four takes later, just as the last light of the day slipped away, *The Tube*'s remake of *Brief Encounter* was finally in the can. 'I think people forget that the films were really pretty once we got into our stride – or once I realised that Geoff would make room for my wildest fantasies,' said Paula. Geoff Wonfor remains a close friend. 'Every kid wanted to be like her. She was amazing. The crap she got in the press – they wouldn't leave her alone and they still won't. But she is sensational. Perfect. And she'll be back.'

Paula and Jools were a director's nightmare... Paula would be on the first floor throwing knickers at him and I'd be trying to get the shot before the light went.

Together, Paula and Jools were a director's nightmare. Occasionally he would lock himself in his room in despair while they misbehaved. 'Jools would be downstairs outside a bar doing a straight piece. Paula would be on the first floor throwing knickers at him and I'd be trying to get the shot before the light went,' said Geoff Wonfor. 'No, you'd always try and get the shot so you could go back and watch the football,' said Paula. 'There was that as well,' he conceded.

It was Paula who interviewed Linda McCartney for a *Tube* film and on the same day posed for the photographer at her studio in Covent Garden. The entire lengthy interview was shot hand-held. By the time the cameraman finally stopped rolling he was exhausted, but the producer still had a few more questions for Linda. Geoff Wonfor was adamant there would be no more filming. 'The cameraman had had enough so I said I wouldn't roll on it,' he said, insisting the rest of the interview be recorded as sound only. As soon as he heard the next question, however, he regretted his decision. 'Paula asked how much Paul actually earns,' he said. 'And Linda said, "Oh, 98.5 pence a second, whether he's asleep or awake" – and I didn't have a camera on it.'

When it came to editing the interview he had to find a way of including this staggering disclosure. His solution was to freeze his final shot of Linda and run the question and answer under a still frame of her face before fading the picture to black. 'Everyone thought it was great, but actually I had no option,' he said.

The Tube's films had none of the stuffiness that prevailed in television at the time.

Members of the crew frequently appeared in shot (and occasionally had the temerity to ask for an appearance fee). Where illusions were created by the magic of television there was every chance the audience would be told.

When Jools interviewed Stevie Winwood the pair were in a car, with the presenter at the wheel. As they meandered along the singer suddenly climbed into the back seat. Seconds later Jools clambered over the driver's seat to join him while the car, miraculously, kept going. The next shot showed it sweeping through the countryside on the back of a low loader surrounded by lights and filming paraphernalia.

On another occasion during a shoot in Liverpool the crew used two cameras – one film and one video – to neatly illustrate the difference between the two mediums. 'We didn't pretend,' said Geoff Wonfor. 'We tried to be as truthful as possible.'

Geoff Wonfor had come to *The Tube* from the BBC, although it was not an easy transition. His wife, Andrea, was head of children's programmes at Tyne Tees as well as executive producer of *The Tube*, and there were strict rules in place to prevent married couples from working together. Producer Malcolm Gerrie fought hard to get the director on board. On his first day, however, Geoff was summoned to the office of the director of programmes. 'You better not be a wanker,' Andy Allen told him. 'Because if you are they'll take you apart.' As it turned out he wasn't, and they didn't.

Often the filming schedules were seemingly impossible. When they set out to make the road movie, *Walking To New Orleans*, as a 90-minute *Tube* special they had just eight days to shoot it. The film featured Fats Domino, Lee Dorsey and a host of other musicians. In the opening few minutes, Sting was seen busking in a subway. And in keeping with the tradition of comedy on *The Tube*, there were cameo appearances from

Robbie Coltrane, Rik Mayall and Stanley Unwin, who gave a wonderfully incomprehensible speech on the history of jazz. In the space of a few days *The Tube* managed to make a movie that truly reflected the musical spirit of New Orleans. 'We managed to capture a lot of people,' said Jools. 'People didn't know about New Orleans music. You could look at that film and you'd have an idea. I think that's important.'

In one of the most precious moments of the film Jools plays boogie-woogie with the legendary Fats Domino. It remains one of the highlights of the entire series. 'We went and visited him in his house and I spent about half an hour explaining the whole film to him and at the end he turned to this guy and said, "I can't understand a word he's saying." He couldn't understand my London accent,' said Jools. 'But there was a piano in the room and his tour manager said just play and then he'll understand what you're on about.' Later, Jools and the crew filmed with Fats Domino in his dressing room at the Festival Hall.

'I think there's something about New Orleans music that's great, there's a truth to it,' said Jools. 'What's particularly incredible about Fats is he's one of the inventors of rock 'n' roll. He really is one of the guvnors of it all.' When they played their duet it was an extraordinary event. 'Jools has the talent and the heart and soul to make you laugh and cry,' said Geoff Wonfor. 'And after that we both cried together.'

Throughout the film Jools was seen driving around Louisiana in a big old battered Oldsmobile. He'd wanted a convertible but rather than hiring one in the conventional manner, the production bought a cheap saloon and performed some crude surgery. Few people realised that the figure in overalls slicing the roof off the car in the film was actually Lee Dorsey. He later popped up in a record store singing the classic 'Working In The Coal Mine'. '*Walking To New Orleans* had a kind of kamikaze, commando feeling,' said Andrea Wonfor. 'It was terrific. They were like a little bunch of terrorists running around.'

Also featured were Rockin' Dopsie And The Cajun Twisters, filmed at the Grant Street dance hall in Lafayette. Their talented blind saxophonist appeared only fleetingly, however, owing to an unfortunate incident during the early stages of the filming. 'In the cameraman's excitement he knocked the poor bloke off the stage,' said Jools. 'The film crew were sometimes marvellously insensitive. I mean they were just a very nice bunch of Newcastle blokes. Perfectly affable blokes you could have a nice beer with afterwards. And there was never any ill or malice to them, but...'

The blind saxophonist incident was by no means the first or last time there was an unfortunate collision between camera and artist. The same thing happened to Mick Jagger during an interview. 'We actually smacked him in the face,' said Geoff Wonfor. Jagger, apparently, took it with good grace.

During a shoot in Birmingham a punk musician with the band Charged GBH ended up with a bloody nose when the cameraman careered into him. 'There was a lot of that, knocking people over,' said Jools. 'Or as soon as it was time to stop they'd stop, even if somebody was in mid-sentence. Just unplug and off we go, thanks a lot.'

One of the more embarrassing incidents took place during a film shoot in LA for the first series of *The Tube*. In 1982 the TV series *Dynasty* was at the height of its popularity and an interview was arranged with one of the stars of the show, Pamela Bellwood. The setting was the palatial Beverly Hills home of the actress. Paula and Pamela sat in the shade at one end of the star's Olympic-size swimming pool. The plan was for the camera to track, gracefully, towards them along the entire length of

Paul McCartney with Leslie Ash and the *Tube* film crew – a very nice bunch of Newcastle blokes

the pool. It was a relatively simple shot, which went horribly wrong. 'She's all dolled up and we're sitting there chatting away and it's very proper,' said Paula. 'The cameraman gets halfway up the pool and shouts, "You'll have to stop – I've pooped my pants!" Well, her face... she just said, "So different, English crews." I never forgot that.'

It was during that same trip that Paula waited patiently for a call from Hollywood superstar Warren Beatty. 'I remember thinking, "I'm on TV, I'm in LA, Warren Beatty will ring me." He rings everyone.' On the last night of the shoot the crew decided to go for an Indian meal while Paula, certain there was still the chance of an eleventh-hour call, stayed in her hotel room. 'The next morning they were all sitting in the hotel lobby looking like they were going to die,' she said, 'and the cameraman's there with this Polaroid, and it's him with his arm round Warren Beatty! They'd met him in the restaurant. I was like, "I can't believe this!"'

Over the years, *The Tube*'s film crew gained access to some of the biggest names in music. Duran Duran threw open the doors of their chateau in the south of France to *The Tube*. Paul McCartney agreed to be interviewed in the back of a black cab as it sped around London – and afterwards signed albums for the crew on the doorstep of his wife's Covent Garden studio. Robert Palmer was interviewed at his home in the Bahamas.

The Tube even filmed underground bands in East Berlin before the wall came down, almost sparking an international incident when the crew piled out of their hire car halfway through Checkpoint Charlie. There was rarely a dull moment. 'We didn't just dash in and do a two-minute interview and dash out again,' said Michael Metcalf, the crew production assistant. 'We built up a relationship with people. They knew they

Despite the
reputation of the
film crew, Robert
Palmer welcomed
them into his home
in the Bahamas

weren't going to be stitched up.'

When Culture Club played in Japan *The Tube* got exclusive, behind-the-scenes footage. The degree of trust Boy George and the band showed Geoff Wonfor on the Japanese shoot was remarkable. Nothing, it seemed, was off limits. From the moment they stepped off their plane and piled into a van the film crew was there, piling in alongside them in a jumble of lights and people. In a sequence of candid interviews Boy George voiced his frustration at his critics. 'How can people call me decadent? – I am the most puritanical person. . . I have never ended a relationship in my life. . . How can anyone hate me?'

As the band prepared for their show in Osaka, Boy George allowed *The Tube* into his dressing room as he applied his trademark make-up. It was the first time such intimacy had been allowed. And, when he went on stage at the packed Castle Stadium, lighting cameraman Graham Brown was right beside him. Just a few months before, Duran Duran's minders had barred the way when *The Tube* tried to take a camera on stage with Simon Le Bon. In terms of access, the Culture Club experience was extraordinary. 'Geoff always got that extra bit from people,' said former researcher Chris Phipps, who was on the Japanese shoot. 'He's not a luvvies director – he's more like a cross between an all-in wrestler and a binman. Completely disarming.'

As was usual with *Tube* films ideas were being thrown around constantly. At short notice it was suggested a traditional teahouse in Osaka would be the ideal setting for a quiet chat with Boy George. Chris Phipps headed off on the Bullet Train to find a suitable location. 'I don't think any of us had had our socks off for about three days we were working so hard,' said Geoff Wonfor. 'I'd slept in my clothes and I remember us all being embarrassed when we had to sit down and have tea in this place and take our shoes off.

I'm sure Jools's feet smelt the worst.' 'He who smelt it dealt it, is all I'd say,' said Jools.

Closer to home, the crew headed for Canvey Island to make a film about a club called the Goldmine. They decided to do some aerial shots and hired a light aircraft. On board was the cameraman, an assistant, the production assistant and Geoff Wonfor. Conditions were cramped and uncomfortable. Since the director was the only one who had seen the club, the others were counting on him to identify it as they flew low over the island. Shortly after take-off, however, he was overcome by acute airsickness. The cameraman, anxious to get his shots, kept filming as Geoff gestured wildly, pointing at the ground. Meanwhile the pilot offered to circle the island again as, in the rear of the tiny plane, the director shook his head. By the time they touched down he was so sick he headed straight to bed.

'It was only when we got back and looked at the aerials that we realised we'd filmed completely the wrong place,' said Michael Metcalf.

The shots were of a giant petrochemical plant on the island. 'When Geoff was pointing down he wasn't pointing at the Goldmine at all – he wanted us to land. It was another shoot that passed into legend.'

Occasional mishaps did nothing to detract from the quality of the films, many of which won international awards. 'The impact was huge and it percolated out into all kinds of things,' said Andrea Wonfor. 'They showed you didn't have to do things in a conventional way.'

(Left) BB King. 'You could tell who were the really great artists because there was much more of a vibe in the room' (This page) Eric Clapton. *The Tube* was a concert with a kind of build-up. Suddenly – Bang! – you were into the live bands at the end of the show

Five: Comic Relief

'You could have a film about Jamaica, a band playing live, and a speciality act like a sword swallower or something.'

Jools Holland

Jools and the irrepressible Dame Edna Everage

IT WAS DURING THE COURSE OF AN OTHERWISE UNEVENTFUL NIGHT at the Tunnel Club, in south London, that Jools spotted an act he thought was perfect for *The Tube*. It featured a man called Les whose imaginative use of a stack of cardboard boxes appeared wholly original. Jools watched, utterly captivated, as Les spent several minutes carefully positioning twenty of the boxes – each one imaginatively crafted to resemble a skyscraper – on the stage. As a finishing touch, tiny lights were placed in each one. 'They looked like the New York skyline,' said Jools, admiringly. 'I was very impressed.'

At this point the opening bars of 'My Kind Of Town' began to play as Les produced two more boxes, which he proceeded to attach to his feet. Lit with torches designed to resemble headlamps, and benefiting from a few additional modifications, the boxes

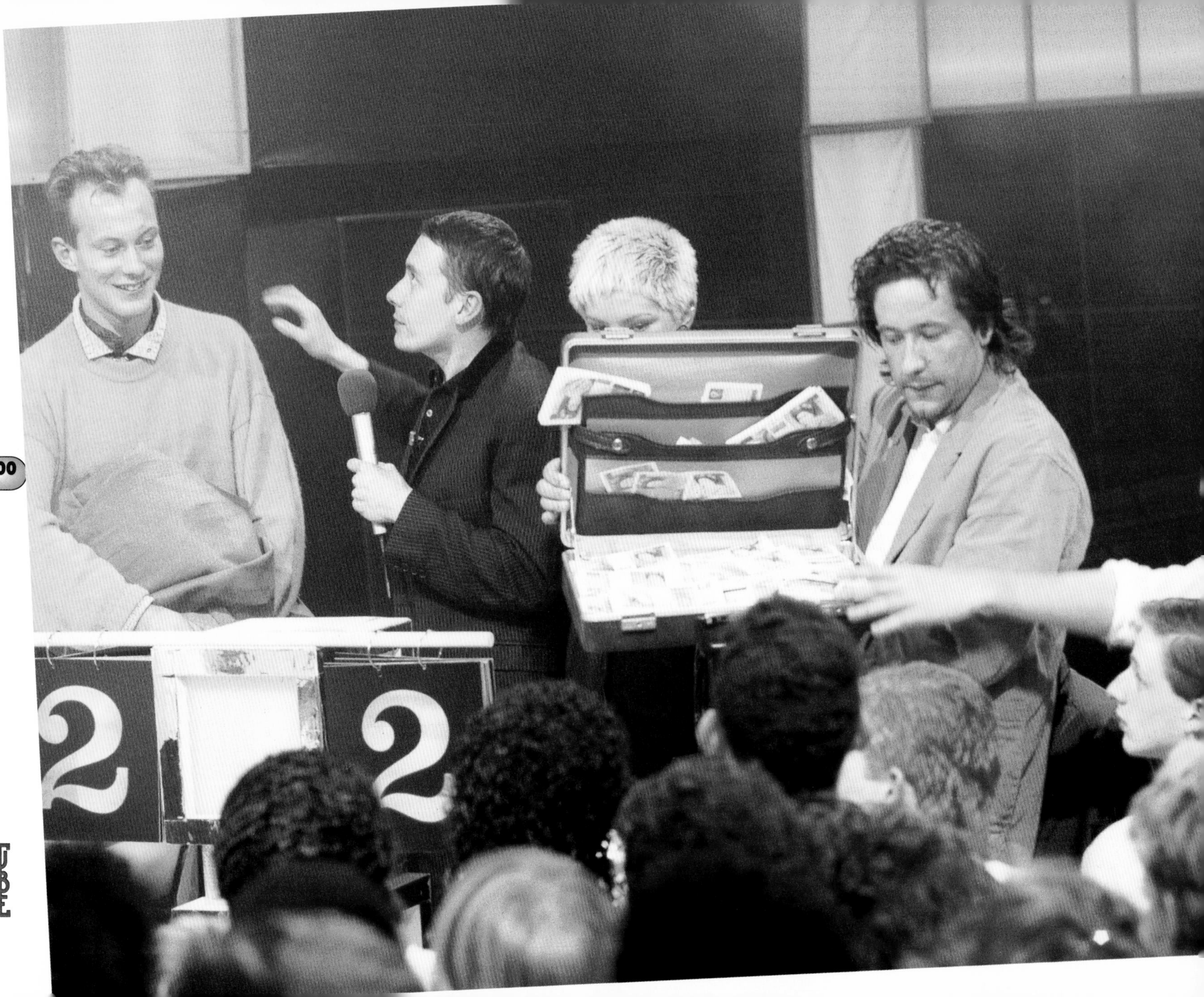
2
2

were transformed into cars. A clumsy but hilarious dance routine ensued. It was just the kind of eccentric performance Jools enjoyed. 'I fell over laughing,' he said. 'I thought it was the most brilliant thing.'

His enthusiasm for the act persuaded *The Tube* producers to book Les and the Amazing Dancing Cars. In no time at all the act was playing on live television before a baffled audience. 'People were completely mystified at this nutter doing this absurd little novelty act on the show,' said Jools, without a trace of regret. 'I could see how some things didn't transfer as well to the screen as others.' When it came to the comedy moments Paula rarely saw eye to eye with Jools. 'I hated all of that,' she said.

It was not so much that Jools went out of his way to find bizarre acts. It just appeared that way. Another of his discoveries was a performer called Edward Barton whose act involved shouting 'I've got a mini car!' over and over, without accompaniment. Even Jools could see that this might not be appropriate to *The Tube*. 'It really was bonkers,' he said.

Then there was Randolph The Remarkable. Randolph, an accomplished if unremarkable fire-eater, revealed a different side entirely on *The Tube*. Bare-chested, his hair concealed beneath a pastel blue shower cap, he belly-flopped into a washing-up bowl on the studio floor. The trick, apparently, was to cause as little spillage as possible on contact with the water. The studio audience gathered round to watch this spectacle with utter bewilderment.

Another comedic tour de force was the man who used to pirouette naked to the tune of 'There's No Business Like Showbusiness' with a Roman Candle up his backside. 'I'd seen this again and again getting a standing ovation because it was such a weird thing,' said Jools. 'I thought, "If it goes down well in these clubs then surely it's got to

Rowland Rivron with a suitcase filled with cash – just one of the prizes no one was likely to win on Square Celebrities

Vic Reeves' first TV appearance. 'I remember thinking "Ooh yeah, I'm a star off the telly" '

102

go down well on our show." I don't think it did
go down very well. But there were other
triumphs.'

   The Tube, with its anything-goes attitude,
proved the perfect platform for a new generation
of so-called alternative comedians. French and
Saunders, Robbie Coltrane, Stephen Fry, Hugh
Laurie and Rik Mayall all made frequent
appearances on the show. 'They weren't about
gags per se,' said Andy Harries, controller of
comedy at Granada TV. 'What other shows could
they appear on apart from *The Tube*? It was hip,
it had the right audience and it had that mad,
anarchic feel.'

   Programmes like *Who Dares Wins* and *The
Comic Strip* were also appearing on Channel 4 –
courtesy of *The Tube*'s commissioning editor,
Mike Bolland. Barry Humphries, in the guise of
Dame Edna Everage, made guest appearances
on *The Tube* and proved entirely at home in the
chaotic atmosphere. Comedy, it seemed, was
the new rock 'n' roll.

   In December, 1986, Vic Reeves made his TV

In the guise of game show host Vic, suspended in a harness high above the studio audience, posed off-the-wall questions to which there were no obvious answers.

To their surprise, it was all a bit low-key. 'There were no shenanigans,' said Norman Pace. 'No **TVs** going out of the windows or anything like that, which was a bit disappointing.'

debut on *The Tube* and was introduced – with great prescience as it turned out – as Britain's top light entertainer. It was the Christmas edition and he hosted a spoof game show called *Square Celebrities*. Guests included Stanley Unwin, Jimmy Nail, TV presenter Sara Hollamby and the newsreader Kenneth Kendall.

Vic was yet another of Jools's discoveries. He had spotted him at Winston's Bar in Deptford, where his stand-up routine revolved around a barmy pub quiz. When Jools caught the show Vic had been in the comedy business for just a matter of weeks. 'I used to do a bit of deejaying and this friend was running a comedy club,' said Vic. 'He asked if I'd take it over and I hadn't the faintest idea who to put on 'cos I didn't know any comedians. So I thought, "Well, I'll do it myself." Six weeks later I was on *The Tube*.'

He was already a fan. Watching *The Tube* was part of his Friday night ritual as he got ready to go boozing with his mates. 'It was quite fantastic really. I thought it was really exciting, the first time I'd been on television. I wasn't particularly nervous but they were all really laid-back. Paula was asleep for about two hours and woke up five minutes before she went on air.'

In the guise of game show host Vic, suspended in a harness high above the heads of the studio audience, posed a series of off-the-wall questions to which there were no obvious answers:

Vic: The long arm of the law is over 16 miles long, but can you tell me the length of Val Doonican's arms?
Sara Hollamby: Well, how long's a piece of string –?
Vic: The answer is an incredible 27 miles long.

Celebrity panelists and contestants alike were bemused. The only certainty about the game was that there was little prospect of the contestants walking away with any of the prizes (although someone did win a waterbed).

Vic, wearing a dinner suit with sequinned lapels, was in his element.

Other than a technical check to make sure his harness was working properly there had been no rehearsals, but he displayed no sign of nerves.

'It was a very good early introduction to television. Being around Jools, you're just having a laugh and it's no big deal. It's good to be around people like that.'

Afterwards, as he flew back to London on the same flight as Womack and Womack,

Rik Mayall and Ade Edmondson (as members of Bad News) with Jools. Comedy was the new rock 'n' roll

who'd played live on the show, it occurred to him that stardom was perhaps not too far away. 'I remember coming back to London and thinking, "Ooh yeah, I'm a star off the telly,"' he said. 'But nobody had actually seen it.'

Former style editor of *Harper's & Queen* magazine Peter York remembers being on one show with a couple of churlish women. 'There were these two rather chubby, bolshie young women standing round and speaking ill of everything,' he said. 'I thought they had been recruited out of a sense of giving token representation to the local talent and I said something like "Who do you think you are?" Of course, they were French and Saunders.'

Hale and Pace were also in the early stages of their career when they were asked to

French and Saunders. 'There were these two rather chubby, bolshie young women standing around and speaking ill of everything...'

As *Brazil* featured a scene in a dentist's chair, Gilliam was to be strapped into a similar chair and 'tortured' into talking about the movie.

guest present while Jools was away on a film shoot. The day before the show they had caught the train up to Newcastle and booked into the Gosforth Park Hotel, expecting to find themselves in the middle of a rock 'n' roll party. To their surprise, it was all a bit low-key. 'There were no shenanigans,' said Norman Pace. 'No TVs going out of the windows or anything like that, which was a bit disappointing.'

The Tube was their first taste of live television and they found themselves right in at the deep end, introducing the show in the guise of the Two Rons from the rooftop car park at Tyne Tees. 'It was terrifying,' said Norman Pace. 'It's just as well it was a mid-shot or you'd have seen my knees knocking. It was quite severe pressure. We weren't sure we'd remember our lines and get through it.'

**Paula and Fifi with
Dame Edna**

The Tube had spotted the comedians doing a stand-up routine at the Tramshed in Woolwich. A spot on *The Tube* represented a major opportunity, but their initial excitement at appearing on the show gave way to mild panic when they arrived at the studios on the day of the show. 'We didn't know who anybody was. There were all these people – researchers, A&R people from record companies. We had no idea who the boss was or who was going to tell us what to do,' said Norman Pace.

Peter York, who made a number of appearances on the show, remembers the atmosphere prior to – and during – transmission well. He said, 'I'm not a very spontaneous human being and I used to wander round and look lost. I thought it doesn't matter – it's not real television – I'm just going to a party. It was like going to a nice club in the north on a Friday evening. You knew it would be alright because you didn't have to wake up the next morning.'

Hale and Pace, meanwhile, settled on a sofa in the Green Room to await instructions. 'Paula came in with Fifi, who was a baby at the time, and a nanny,' said Norman Pace. 'It was obvious that she was the queen of the show. She just plonked herself down between us. She actually sat directly on us and we had to make room for her.'

As the hours ticked by a horrible realisation dawned. The formal briefing they were expecting was unlikely to happen. During rehearsals they were given white gowns and told to interview director Terry Gilliam, who was on the show to promote *Brazil*, his first feature film. 'We wanted our questions from the researcher but he was so laid-back he wouldn't give them to us,' said Norman Pace. 'He said he wanted to get to know us a bit better before working out what he wanted to say.'

As *Brazil* featured a scene in a dentist's chair, Gilliam was to be strapped into a similar chair and 'tortured' into talking about the movie.

The comedians were understandably nervous. During rehearsals Norman, whose instrument of torture was a vacuum cleaner, almost caused a catastrophe when he poked the appliance into the director's mouth and attached it to a tooth. Gilliam was not amused. 'He said, "Jesus Christ, I haven't come all the way to Newcastle to get my teeth knocked out by some third-rate comedian,"' said Norman Pace. 'I think he was being generous –'

To everyone's relief, the torture sequence went off without a hitch on transmission. Afterwards no one mentioned the unfortunate incident with the vacuum cleaner. 'We travelled back to London on the train with Terry Gilliam and he seemed to have forgiven me,' said Norman Pace. 'But you know, he never kept in touch and he didn't cast us in any of his movies, so who knows?'

Love Wars on stage: Womack and Womack

111

Six: Those Groovy Effers

IT WAS ON A CHILLY NOVEMBER NIGHT IN 1984 that *The Tube* managed to pull off one of its more infamous openings. Not that it was planned or scripted. As far as the producers were concerned, there was nothing shocking or offensive in that night's line-up. Grandmaster Melle Mel, The Alarm, Shriekback, Billy Bragg and left-wing skinhead band the Redskins were playing live. There was an interview with Duran Duran, recorded in the south of France. And the style commentator Peter York had come along to discuss picture discs and designer stubble. Yet within seconds of going on air complaints were already lighting up the Channel 4 switchboard.

The first thing viewers saw was a dishevelled Rik Mayall stumble drunkenly out of the Egypt Cottage pub next to the studio and vomit on the pavement. Groans of disgust could be heard coming from the audience queuing at the entrance to the studio a few yards away.

Rik, in a gaudy green jacket and pink open-necked shirt, his right hand heavily bandaged, swayed about unsteadily as he delivered his opening line. 'It's Friday, it's half-past five and the pubs are open. My name's thingy and –' he gestured towards

[and other famous slip-ups]

the studio '– this is the tunnel, the hole, er, thing.' In the production gallery, director Gavin Taylor cursed under his breath and rolled the opening titles.

One outraged viewer in Oxford called the police. 'I don't know what he thought they were going to do,' said Jools. 'Send a squad car over straight away?' Throughout the show Rik kept up the running gag, lurching onto set and disrupting an interview with Peter York. 'I don't remember that at all,' says Peter York now. 'I think you were so prepared for anything to happen that you barely noticed.'

Later, Jools was seen looking for Rik in his dressing room. 'Britain's number one comedian,' he said cheerfully, opening the door to find Rik slumped over the sink in a pool of vomit, a stack of empties beside him. 'You're a bad example to young people,' he said, dragging him away.

Rik finally made it onto stage, his nose bloodied, to deliver just one line. 'Good evening,' he said, with perfect timing, as the Tyne Tees production slide appeared. The show was over. In the background Jools could be heard saying, 'Oh, he appears to have passed out –'

'I do think that any time there was trouble it was always amusing. That was the point of it.'

Jools Holland

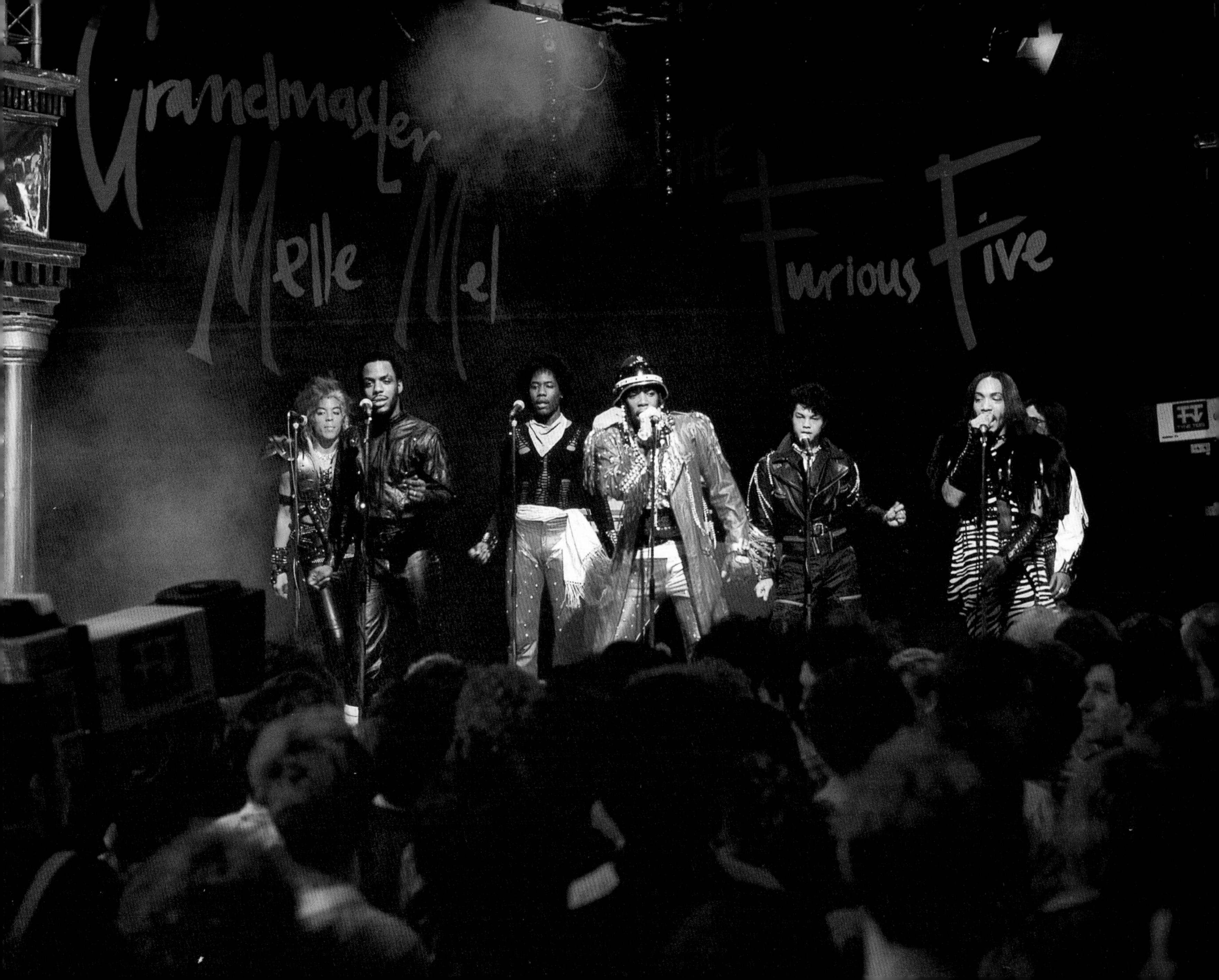
Grandmaster
Melle Mel
THE
Furious Five

Grandmaster Melle Mel and the Furious Five. Great music, shame about the fashion

It was during that same show, in the middle of a set by the Redskins, that there was another unrehearsed incident. On to the stage walked a Durham miner who'd been on strike for 35 weeks, to deliver a message to the government. As luck would have it he chose a mike that wasn't working and consequently his protest speech went unheard.

Predictably, there was an outcry. Critics, convinced the plug had been pulled deliberately, rounded on *The Tube* for supposed censorship. 'Some of the things we got into trouble for were hilarious and nothing to do with us,' said Chris Cowey, referring to the Redskins incident. 'I'm sure he was a great miner but he wasn't a great rock 'n' roll star. He just picked the wrong mike.'

It was an eventful show for the Redskins. Later on they got into a fight with a man called Thor who specialised in blowing up hot-water bottles until they burst. 'It was all just a bit sad,' said Jools.

Complaints about bad behaviour on *The Tube* began during the first series and were often prompted by innocuous remarks. On one occasion Jools, giving details of a poster offer, brandished a perspex tube saying, 'We were going to have a competition and have lots of hamster

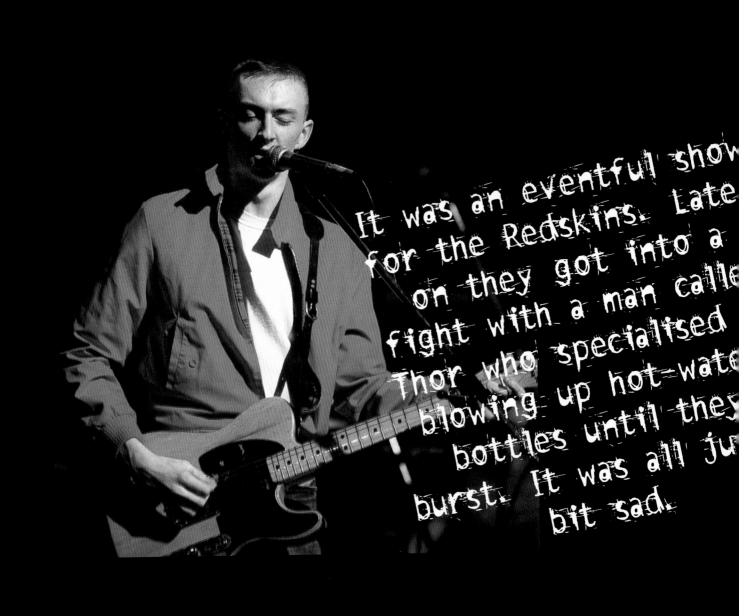

It was an eventful show for the Redskins. Late on they got into a fight with a man called Thor who specialised blowing up hot-water bottles until they burst. It was all ju bit sad.

turds in here and the one that guessed how many there were would get a free poster.' Pausing briefly, he added, 'We'll have some more letters about that.'

A week later he confirmed there had indeed been complaints. Unrepentant, he urged the audience to write in and nominate the rude words they'd most like to hear on *The Tube*. 'The best suggestion will be accepted,' he said.

After the first few shows the Independent Broadcasting Authority, as it then was, set up a watchdog to pay close attention to *The Tube*'s content. 'There was the week when Jools said Michael Jackson's got a hamster called Willy and the competition this week is how big is Michael Jackson's Willy,' recalled former executive producer Andrea Wonfor. 'That got us a reprimand in writing.'

'They were harmless little word puns, I thought,' said Jools. 'A little bit of double entendre, a little bit of innuendo. I do think that any time there was trouble it was always amusing. That was the point of it.'

On another show, Jools introduced the inventor of a new musical instrument called a rhythm stick, worn slung round the neck like a guitar but without strings. It was a neat, if peculiar-looking, electronic synthesiser. During rehearsals it had remained switched off, so the presenter was unprepared for the noise it made once it was powered up. He reacted, understandably, with a four-letter expletive. 'There wasn't a single complaint about that 'cos nobody noticed, it was so quick,' he said.

From time to time there was talk of making *The Tube* a recorded show, which the production team were determined would not happen. As long as it was live it retained an element of surprise, which the audience loved.

Strongman Thor explains his fascination with hot-water bottles to Leslie Ash

117

Dexy's Midnight Runners. Not only were bands prepared to go to Newcastle, they were also prepared to play live

Jools paid scant attention to the complaints that trickled in. 'I remember one producer saying we'd had four letters of complaint and that each letter in television represents the views of a thousand people. I said one letter means one nutter's bothered to write in. That was my view at the time.'

Studio director Gavin Taylor often found himself the lone dissenting voice on the production team. 'I was often the killjoy,' he said. 'Maybe I was too conservative. Everyone was looking for the outrageous and I was the one who'd say that's abysmal and disgusting.'

Just two weeks after the Rik Mayall incident there was another controversial opening when Jools and Paula introduced the show from the dressing room corridor. 'And this is dressing room 3,' said Paula. 'Which is Lords Of The New Church,' said Jools. 'And let's burst in on them.' Throwing open the door, they revealed singer Stiv Bators, bare-chested with a pair of jeans in his hand. He flung the jeans aside to give viewers a full frontal flash. 'Oh dear, and bursting out again all in a hurry,' said Jools, hurriedly closing the dressing room door. 'Well, it's a live show and you get to see a lot of live things,' said Paula, barely able to contain her laughter.

It was frequently the guests, rather than the presenters, who landed *The Tube* in hot water. On one show, comic Mel Smith appeared with Jimmy Nail to promote their new film, *Morons From Outer Space*. Fish and chips had been provided but Jimmy Nail was unimpressed. Holding up a soggy-looking fish he declared, 'This is worse than the fucking Beeb.'

Paul Young's first appearance on *The Tube* also provoked a reprimand from

'In my mind I
was thinking to
myself, "be there or
be..." And I thought,
I'm not going to say
square, because what
a stupid thing that
would be to say.'

tongue,' said Jools. 'In my mind I was slowly thinking to myself, be there or be... And I thought, I'm not going to say square because what a stupid thing that would be to say.'

Following his suspension Jools returned to the studio and promptly expressed his gratitude to the many people – Paul McCartney, Kate Bush and Sir Reg Kray among them – who had taken the time to send letters of support. His tongue remained firmly in his cheek. 'There was a certain amount of couldn't care less about it all. It was "Oh fuck, it doesn't matter,"' said Jools.

'He thrived in the zoo atmosphere of *The Tube*,' said style commentator Peter York. 'I think they were very lucky in having somebody as self-confident and singular as Julian.'

'It was never really stated by any of us, but I think it was part of the policy to skate close to the edge of being in trouble. That was the only way *The Tube* could have its attitude,' said Chris Cowey. '*The Tube* ran for five years with more than 20 shows a year

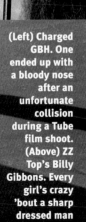

(Left) Charged GBH. One ended up with a bloody nose after an unfortunate collision during a Tube film shoot. (Above) ZZ Top's Billy Gibbons. Every girl's crazy 'bout a sharp dressed man

It was part of the policy to skate close to the edge of being in trouble. That was the only way *The Tube* could have its attitude

ls with Stevie Wonder
ft) and Little Richard.
'Jools had a wonderful
ocking deadpan cool –
and he could play'

and, considering we encouraged free-wheeling behaviour and live performances, it didn't go badly wrong,' said Andrea Wonfor.

It was midway through the fifth series that Tyne Tees issued a statement to say *The Tube* had run its course. Paula Yates and Muriel Gray presented the final programme on 24 April 1987. Live in the studio were The Cure, 14 Karat Soul, Mel And Kim, and Duran Duran. James Brown, who was to have appeared, pulled out at short notice. 'Originally we heard it was because he'd been shot, which is a pretty cool soul-singer kind of thing,' said Paula. 'Then we heard he'd had 144 stitches in his mouth because one of his false teeth went rotten... Not very cool.'

Jools appeared in his last ever *Tube* film, a spoof shopping extravaganza with Rowland Rivron and Hugh Laurie. Rowland, in soiled vest and long johns – reminiscent of Jool's own inherited lucky pants – sportingly slipped into a selection of ill-fitting outfits in pursuit of a new, fashionable image. With Hugh Laurie as the shop assistant from hell, there was little prospect of success.

There were farewell messages from Tina Turner, Paul Young, Boy George and U2. 'Channel 4, damn you,' said Boy George. 'I'm a big Jools Holland fan and I like Paula Yates. I've never

Duran Duran – always one of Paula's favourites – closed the show. She introduced them from an upturned crate with Muriel at her side.

Former Labour leader Neil Kinnock
arrived at Tyne Tees to do a local news
show – and found himself at *The Tube*

had sex with her, though.' Paul Young said, 'This is it lads. I thought I'd say thanks very much to everybody who worked on *The Tube*. It gave me my big break.'

Duran Duran – always one of Paula's favourites – closed the show. She introduced them from an upturned crate with Muriel at her side. In the final moments of *The Tube* the lack of chemistry between the two was apparent. 'You're standing on a box, that's cheating,' said Muriel, as the camera tilted down to reveal the reason for Paula's sudden height advantage. 'I can see right down your enormous cleavage – it's huge!' Paula rolled her eyes as Muriel dissolved in giggles. 'We have possibly the greatest band to finish,' said Paula. Muriel moved close and pulled a face. Paula pushed her away. 'Don't get any closer, Muriel – this isn't hot lesbo action time,' she said.

Gavin Taylor directed the final show with an air of disbelief. 'Suddenly it was over and done with and I couldn't believe it,' he said. 'A lot of people were very shocked. I don't think anyone ever came up with a good enough reason for ending it.'

(Left) Jimmy Somerville
(Right) Marc Almond

The Cure played the final *Tube*. 'It was a heady cocktail that night'

Malcolm Gerrie is adamant that the time was right to call it a day. He wanted *The Tube* to go out – just as it launched – with a bang. 'We all wanted to end it then. I didn't want it to fizzle out and grow really tired,' he said. Once the final show was over the celebrations began. There had been many *Tube* parties before but none perhaps where such an air of abandonment prevailed. 'I remember not going to bed for 48 hours,' said Malcolm Gerrie. 'The party just went on and on. We'd booked a restaurant down on the quayside and we ended up back there the following night – we were still going strong.'

The Thompson
Twins

Emotions were running high. Someone leapt off the Tyne Bridge wearing a *Tube*
T-shirt. When the party shifted to the Tuxedo Princess, a floating nightclub on the
river, the police were called. 'There was a whole bunch of *Tube* personnel who were
well out of order,' recalled Gerrie cheerfully.

Beneath the carousing, however, lay a deep sense of loss among those for whom *The
Tube* had become a way of life for five glorious years. 'There was sadness on lots of
different levels because it marked the start of a real decline for Tyne Tees,' said Gerrie.

(Above, left) Howard Jones (Above, right) Lee John and Imagination (Opposite) Mel & Kim on the final *Tube*

'To see such a vibrant station going pear-shaped and to see the break-up of a crack team was terrible... It was a heady cocktail that night – both in terms of alcohol and emotions.'

The years following the demise of *The Tube* have seen major changes at Tyne Tees. The second floor of the studio complex, which once housed the show's production offices and the artists' Green Room, is now the management zone. 'It's very funny going back now,' said Andrea Wonfor. 'It's all thick carpet and the boardroom's there.'

An air of tranquillity has replaced the frenetic atmosphere once generated by *The Tube*. Although not for much longer, perhaps. There are those who believe the time is right for *The Tube* to rise, phoenix-like, from the ashes. 'There's a great club scene, some great bands around and others coming through,' said Andrea Wonfor. 'How do you find something that maybe you call *Tube 2000* or whatever, which reflects all that and has

its own persona and does something different? The challenge is to see if we can bottle something out of the zeitgeist of 1999 and into 2000 and make it work.' '*The Tube* was enormously influential in galvanising what was going on musically in the early to mid-Eighties,' said Paul Young's former manager, Ged Doherty. 'I think there's a huge gap now for that kind of programme.'

For Trevor Horn, who produced the hit single 'Relax' after spotting Frankie Goes To Hollywood on *The Tube*, there has been no obvious successor to the show. 'There isn't a TV programme that could make anybody's career at the moment. And *The Tube* did make a few careers – not just the Frankies,' he said.

The final word goes to Jools, whose five years on *The Tube* taught him one basic – but vital – rule of presenting. 'I suppose I must have introduced a thousand artists on camera and the one thing I did learn is that you always say the name last,' he said. 'In endless television programmes it's amazing the number of people who don't know that's what you have to do. So they'll say the person's name, then everyone applauds, and nobody can hear what they say afterwards. 'It's one of the simplest things – and it's the only thing I learnt on *The Tube*.' Now that's impressive.

Courtney Pine and the Jazz Messengers

Stiv Bators and Lords of the New Church. *The Tube* encouraged incendiary characters

139

Suddenly it was over
couldnt believe it
were very

and done with and I
A lot of people
shocked.

141